PLAIN AND SIMPLE

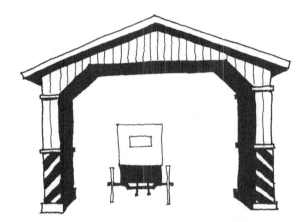

PLAIN AND SIMPLE

A Woman's Journey to the Amish

SUE BENDER

Illustrations by
Sue Bender and Richard Bender

HarperOne
An Imprint of HarperCollins*Publishers*

HarperOne

HarperCollins Web site: http://www.harpercollins.com

HarperCollins®, 📕®, and HarperOne™ are trademarks of HarperCollins Publishers.

FIRST HARPERCOLLINS PAPERBACK EDITION PUBLISHED IN 1991

Library of Congress Cataloging-in-Publication Data

Bender, Sue
    Plain and simple : a woman's journey to the Amish / Sue Bender; illustrations by Sue Bender and Richard Bender. — 1st HarperCollins paperback edition.
    p. cm.
    ISBN: 978–0–06–250186–8
1. Self-actualization (Psychology)—Case studies. 2. Amish—Social life and customs—Psychological aspects. 3. Simplicity. I. Title.
BF637.S4B44   1989
305.6'87—dc20   89–45234

HB 07.14.2021

To Richard, Michael, and David—whom I love.

CONTENTS

PLAIN AND SIMPLE

Throughout this work, proper names, place names, and identifying details have been changed to ensure the privacy of those involved.

PROLOGUE

I had an obsession with the Amish. Plain and simple. Objectively it made no sense. I, who worked hard at being special, fell in love with a people who valued being ordinary.

When I told people I wanted to live with an Amish family everybody laughed. "Impossible," they said. "No Amish family will take you in."

I didn't know when I first looked at an Amish quilt and felt my heart pounding that my soul was starving, that an inner voice was trying to make sense of my life.

I didn't know that I was beginning a journey of the spirit, what Carlos Castaneda calls following "a path that has heart."

I thought I was going to learn more about their quilts, but the quilts were only guides, leading me to what I really needed to learn, to answer a question I hadn't formed yet:

"Is there another way to lead a good life?"

I went searching in a foreign land and found my way home.

Perhaps each of us has a starved place, and each of us knows deep down what we need to fill that place. To find the courage to trust and honor the search, to follow the voice that tells us what we need to do, even when it doesn't seem to make sense, is a worthy pursuit. This story is about that search.

Maybe you have a dream, incubating, not fully formed. Maybe you are on a similar quest. I hope you will listen to my story and at the same time hear yours. That way it will be our journey.

CHAPTER ONE

How It Began

Can an object go straight to your heart ?

1

Twenty years ago I walked into Latham's Men's Store in Sag Harbor, New York, and saw old quilts used as a background for men's tweeds. I had never seen quilts like that. Odd color combinations. Deep saturated solid colors: purple, mauve, green, brown, magenta, electric blue, red. Simple geometric forms: squares, diamonds, rectangles. A patina of use emanated from them. They spoke directly to me. They knew something. They went straight to my heart.

That was the beginning. Innocent enough.

"Who made these quilts?" I demanded.

"The Amish."

I went back to Latham's every day that summer, as if in a trance, not noticing it at first, just something I did in the midst of all the other things I was doing. Visiting the quilts became a practice, something like a spiritual practice, the one constant in days that were otherwise filled with the activities of summer.

I stared at the quilts. They seemed so silent: a "silence like thunder." It was 1967, and I was thirty-three years old.

I had seen lots of old quilts before, made by non-Amish women. They drew on an unlimited palette: plaid, polka dots, calico, corduroy, velvet. Their patterns were endless: Geese in Flight, Log Cabin, Bear Paw, Fans, Pinwheel, School House, Broken Dishes, Old Maid's Puzzle, Indian Hatchet, Crown of Thorns, and many more.

The Amish used the same few patterns over and over—no need to change the pattern, no need to make an individual statement.

The basic forms were tempered by tiny, intricate black quilting stitches. The patterns—tulips, feathers, wreaths, pineapples, and stars—softened and complemented the hard lines, and the contrast of simple pattern and complex stitchery gave the flat, austere surface an added dimension. I wondered if quilting was an acceptable way for a woman to express her passion?

I learned that the Amish used their old clothing to make the haunting colors in the quilts. Nothing was wasted; out of the scrap pile came those wondrous saturated colors. Like most deeply religious farm people, the Amish wore dark, solid-colored clothing, made from homespun material. But underneath, hidden from view, were brightly colored petticoats, blouses, and shirts.

Colors of such depth and warmth were combined in ways I had never seen before. At first the colors looked somber, but then—looking closely at a large field of brown—I discovered that it was really made up of small patches of many different shades and textures of color. Greys and shiny dark and dull light brown, dancing side by side, made the flat surface come alive. Lush greens lay beside vivid reds. An electric blue appeared as if from nowhere on the border.

The relationship of the individual parts to the whole, the proportion, the way the inner and outer borders reacted with each other was a balancing act between tension and harmony.

The quilts spoke to such a deep place inside me that I felt them reaching out, trying to tell me something, but my mind was thoroughly confused. How could pared-down and daring go together? How could a quilt be calm and intense at the same time? Can an object do that? Can an object know something?

. . .

How opposite my life was from an Amish quilt.

My life was like a CRAZY QUILT, a pattern I hated. Hundreds of scattered, unrelated, stimulating fragments, each going off in its own direction, creating a lot of frantic energy. There was no overall structure to hold the pieces together. The Crazy Quilt was a perfect metaphor for my life.

A tug-of-war was raging inside me.

In contrast to the muted colors of the Amish, I saw myself in extremes: a black-and-white person who made black-and-white ceramics and organized her life around a series of black-and-white judgments.

I divided my world into two lists. All the "creative" things—the things I valued, being an artist, thinking of myself as undisciplined and imaginative—were on one side, and the boring, everyday things—those deadly, ordinary chores that everyone has to do, the things I thought distracted me from living an artistic life—were on the other side.

I was an ex-New Yorker living most of the time in Berkeley, California; a wife and mother of two sons; an artist and a therapist with two graduate degrees, one from Harvard, one from Berkeley. That was my resume.

I valued accomplishments.

I valued being special.

I valued results.

The driven part didn't question or examine these values. It took them as real, and believed it was following the carrot "success" wholeheartedly. Didn't everyone believe in success? I never asked, "Success at what cost?"

A part of me is quiet. It knows about simplicity, about commitment, and the joy of doing what I do well. That part is the artist, the child—it is receptive and has infinite courage. But time and my busyness drowned the quiet voice.

In the world in which I grew up, more choices meant a better life.

It was true for both my parents and my grandparents. I was brought up to believe that the more choices I had, the better.

Never having enough time, I wanted it all, a glutton for new experience. Excited, attracted, distracted, tempted in all directions, I thought I was lucky to have so many choices and I naively believed I could live them all.

A tyranny of lists engulfed me. The lists created the illusion that my life was full.

I would wake at five A.M. eager to begin. The first thing I did was to compose my *Things to Do* list. This gave me great pleasure, even though the list was nothing more than a superimposed heap of choices, representing all the things I enjoyed doing and all the things I had to do, crowding and bumping against each other. Any organized person would have said "This is ridiculous. It's unrealistic. No one could accomplish so many things in one day."

Sometimes I would stop in the middle of the day, when the scene on the page looked especially chaotic, and rewrite the list, never thinking to take anything off, but hoping the newly transformed neat rows would overcome my feeling of being overwhelmed. It was a balancing act on one foot—even when I was doing something I enjoyed, my mind jumped about, thinking of what was next on my list.

I never thought to stop and ask myself, "What really matters?" Instead, I gave everything equal weight. I had no way to select what was important and what was not. Things that were important didn't get done, and others, quite unimportant, were completed and crossed off the list.

Accumulating choices was a way of not having to make a choice, but I didn't know that at the time. To eliminate anything was a foreign concept. I felt deprived if I let go of any choices.

By evening, the list had become a battlefield of hieroglyphics; crossed-off areas, checks and circles, plus the many temptations added during the day. The circles were there to remind me of all the tasks that didn't get done. Tomorrow's list began with today's leftovers.

I never questioned my frantic behavior. When I looked around, most of my friends were like me, scurrying around and complaining that they never had the time to do all the things they really wanted to do.

Only now, looking back, can I hear a child's voice inside me calling "*STOP*, I want to get off. The merry-go-round is spinning faster and faster. Please make it stop."

At the time I thought I was extremely lucky. But something was missing, and though I could not have said what that "something" was, I was always searching, believing there was *something out there* —and if only I could find it. That "if only" kept me trying to change. I took classes—trying to improve, hoping I'd be a better person. A friend laughed, "I'll know you've changed when you stop trying to change."

I didn't know that my addiction to unrelenting activity produced a quiet desperation that permeated every cell of my being. In the world of "if only," nothing I was doing would ever be enough.

Spinning frantically, I left myself out.

. . .

I had become an artist by chance.

In 1960, three months before the birth of my first child, I stopped teaching history at New Rochelle High School in New York and joined a clay class. The timing was perfect: I had planned to miss only three months of teaching before school began again in September. I never returned. In those few months, I fell in love with clay. Clay was soft and responsive. It had its own rhythm, its own heartbeat, a timing sensitive to moods and the atmosphere, just like a person. It didn't make demands, but it did ask me to pay attention and to listen. I thought being receptive meant being "out of control," so I had a lot of difficulty with that part of the relationship. On damp days, the clay took longer to harden. Impatient, I put the pieces in my kitchen oven, willing them to dry faster.

For all the abuse I gave the clay, I also had a natural connection with the material. Clay became part of me, not just something I did. But I never saw myself as just a potter. Refusing to make regular or practical forms, I felt I was something more, an *artist.* To me "regular" meant ordinary. I was determined to stand out.

Growing up in New York, my parents' message had been *"Be a Star,"* though these words were never said out loud. The first things I made were beautiful, shining ceramic stars, with real gold luster. I loved making them. The child in me was still dreaming of becoming a star.

I spent many years in school. Achieve, achieve, I heard, and along with the words came a clear picture of the right way to be. Even the air I breathed seemed to agree. Clay was different. It was flexible, encouraging me to take a chance.

I tried to learn the potter's wheel but I resisted its discipline and was singularly unsuccessful at using it. To explain my ineptness, I told myself I was afraid I would get hooked on the technology of the wheel, and end up making perfectly thrown, characterless pots. I never understood that while the clay was whirling around on the wheel, centering a pot meant centering myself. At that time I was too scattered to find that calm inner focus.

In the summer of 1967, I had my first show.

The pieces were impractical, fanciful objects and whimsical creatures from my imagination. *"More, more!"* my demons demanded, for in their world "more" meant better. It was a year of hell. Instead of enjoying the work, I pushed myself, trying to make each piece more original than the previous one. The more I willfully tried to force something fresh, the more I failed. Never pausing to take a breath, I raced around on full power until, exhausted, I finally caved in. Only then, when my frantic pace was temporarily halted, could I make pieces I felt good about.

At the opening of my show people came up to greet me.

"You must be such a happy person. Your work is so filled with fun," said one guest.

"If I made ceramics that looked the way I felt this year, the work would be gnarled and hideous," I replied.

■   ■   ■

Each time I went back to look at them that summer, those stoic Amish quilts with their spartan shapes, sent shock waves through me—a grown woman mesmerized. These are dramatic words, but that's what it felt like. The connection was immediate and electric.

My busyness stopped. The fragments of my life became still. I was coming home, connecting to a part of me that I had ignored, even depreciated. I felt calm.

CHAPTER TWO

The Ninepatch and the Faceless Dolls

A few months after my show, in the fall of 1967, we moved to California, but kept our summer home on Long Island. The ceramic show had been a success, but I didn't feel like one. Then, one day, a line in the Berkeley High School Adult Education newsletter announcing an Amish quilting class caught my eye. I was busy with wall-to-wall commitments, but something propelled me to that classroom.

13

It made no sense. I loved old Amish quilts, but I could barely sew. I didn't know how to thread a bobbin nor did I wish to learn. My grandfather had been a tailor and my mother had said, "Don't bother with practical things." I wasn't the domestic type. To tell the truth, I didn't value women who were domestic.

But I walked into a classroom at Berkeley High School and joined twenty-nine women whose passion was quilting. What was I doing there?

Our first assignment was to make a "ninepatch" using Amish colors. A ninepatch is the simplest quilting pattern, the one an Amish mother uses to initiate her daughter into the craft of quilt making. In theory, the concept is easy. Place one dark square next to one light square, until a grid of nine patches comes together in a tic-tac-toe pattern.

I started moving the squares around. Then around some more.

Surrounded by the colors of the Amish—deep purples, greys, mauves, magentas, and blacks—I sat on my bedroom floor, watching "Love Boat" on television. But the pieces seemed wrong, too new, too much like an interior designer's good taste. I had to intrude on the newness. I boiled coffee and rubbed it into the cloth. I added tea. I found some India ink and tried that. The next day I went out and bought Rit dye. I wanted the material to look old, to feel old. I wanted the squares to evoke a sense of history, to be stripped down, bare, essential. I wanted to recapture the feeling I had when I looked at an old Amish quilt, to re-create the haunting spiritual quality that seemed to come from deep inside the quilt.

I put together nine groups of nine patches and moved them around until they seemed to know on their own where they belonged. Torn and ragged, the colors, now muted, blemished, used and abused, at last had patina. These rich, saturated pieces united me with the Amish and with myself.

Each week, twenty-nine women showed their small, beautifully crafted, completed quilts, and each week I brought in another ancient-looking fragment, awkwardly sewn and borderless. I felt that my quilt fragments had to remain open, for whatever might happen.

■　■　■

A few years later, at the Whitney Museum, I saw a show of old Americana quilts. The ones from Lancaster County, Pennsylvania, stood out. Hung flat on white walls, these minimalist, austere quilts looked like strong, modern American paintings and seemed completely at ease in their new setting. The art world opened its eyes and relabeled the quilts: art.

I kept asking myself, how do these farm women make such forceful works of art? Very few people knew about Amish quilts back then, but I finally met a quilt dealer who had lived among the Amish in Lancaster County. He told me, "No one is labeled an 'artist' in an Amish community. That would be a sign of false pride. They're a deeply religious people, and humility is a trait that's valued. Things are made to be used, not revered."

How opposite I was from the Amish!

I was proud to think of myself as an artist with a capital *A*.

■ ■ ■

Preparing for my first show had taught me that when I tried to *perform*, my worry over the outcome robbed me of my joy in simply doing the work. I decided to keep my art separate from a career. Going back to an earlier interest, I enrolled at age forty, in the psychiatric social work program at Berkeley. At that time, mid-life was still the neglected stepchild of the life cycle, so when I graduated, I invited friends to join me, and set up a program for mid-life women. I called it CHOICE.

College professors, homemakers, artists, real estate agents, and a bus driver from Oakland came together in a group called "Warriors of the Spirit." Each was struggling to find a way to balance divergent and demanding roles—career woman, homemaker, mother, divorcée, wife, lover, single parent, friend.

How to fuse the disparate choices into one life? How to design a life with all the varied pieces—arrange and rearrange—and in the process create a feasible pattern to live by?

I didn't have answers for them, or for myself, but I thought the search for the answers was important.

. . .

Though I never thought of buying an Amish quilt, I spent the next years searching for them. Quilt dealers who knew of my growing interest called when they returned from buying trips. Each time I made a pilgrimage to see them, I returned home calm. My head was filled with questions. What was the intention of the woman as she began making a quilt for her daughter? Was her life embodied in her quilt? Was she telling me something of her hopes and dreams?

Many years after I had seen my first Amish quilt, in the fall of 1981, I walked into Ed Brown's Folk Art Gallery in San Francisco and saw three strange-looking dolls that had no features drawn on them—the eyes, noses, mouths, fingers, and toes were missing. One was stuffed with straw, another with quilt batting, and the third with rags. Their bodies were covered with hardy unbleached muslin. Dressed in tattered, dark, old-fashioned clothing and bonnets, they were quite unlike the pink doll babies I had known as a child. Like voodoo dolls, they cast their spell.

Astounded, I asked Ed Brown, "Where do these odd dolls come from?"

"The Amish."

"Why are their faces blank?" I asked.

"The rule comes from their religion," he said. "The Bible says, 'Thou shalt not make any graven image, or any likeness of anything that is in heaven above, or that is in the earth beneath.'"

For generations Amish mothers have made these dolls for their daughters. Always the same, no need to change or embellish or improve them. They just need to be durable enough to withstand lots of use.

I stood looking at these three old tattered dolls, and each week I went back to stare at them. On the surface they looked the same, but when I looked closer, each one had a distinct personality, the unique mark of the mother who made the doll for her child. Finally, just looking at the dolls wasn't enough. Thinking about the dolls, daydreaming about the quilts, I realized I had to know more. Back in New York that summer my husband and I, tourists like everyone else, drove off to Lancaster County, Pennsylvania, to visit the Amish.

What we saw wasn't quaint, make-believe Williamsburg, nor a re-enactment of country living in the nineteenth century. These people weren't acting. They were quietly minding their own business as they drove their neatly painted black horse-drawn buggies down the narrow country lanes. The Amish call those people who aren't Amish the "English" (the "other sort of people"). We "English" were creating a traffic hazard, stopping to take their pictures.

If the Amish were bothered by the intrusion of these gaping English outsiders, they didn't show it. Although they were a major attraction for masses of aggressive, curious tourists, they moved around unhurried, as if in a contemplative world of their own. Their somber expression, staring straight ahead, their faces encased in large black bonnets—all this created an atmosphere that made me uncomfortable.

Surrounded by grossly commercial motels, neon signs flashing "Plain and Fancy," the Amish had created a world in sharp contrast. The fields looked like their quilts—rich, lush, orderly, and serene.

This was their world, and we were voyeurs, looking at them with the same curiosity we might look at someone in a freak show. I hated it—and had to leave. "Are there any Amish communities where the people don't live in a fish bowl?" I asked the surprised woman at the tourist bureau. She suggested a somewhat remote county several hours away, in Ohio.

We left small country roads for even smaller lanes, meandering with no plan, leaving behind the world of road markers. That was unusual for us, getting unhooked from the world of road maps and certainty.

I was looking for an excuse to begin a conversation, so when we arrived I began asking Amish women if they could tell me where the nearest Amish dry goods store was, saying I wanted to buy a faceless doll and some solid colored cotton material.

The stores were hard to find, tucked away on back-country roads, looking like every other Amish house, a white wooden building with black trim, no sign outside. After a while I could spot them by the hitching posts and buggies standing outside. I learned to recognize Amish homes by the absence of electrical wires leading to the

house. Several homes used windmills, but the easiest clue was the clothesline, full of trousers and blouses in dark, vibrant Amish colors, hung neatly on the line in order of size.

"Do you sell faceless dolls?" I would ask.

"No, we don't sell them," I was told everywhere. "Every mother makes her own doll."

"Do you know anyone who might be willing to make a doll for me?"

Finally, lost on a small country lane, we met an old woman who sold a few basic sewing supplies from a room in the back of her house. "You can try down the road. The two sisters who live there are midwives and I think they make dolls for the new babies."

We found the house. "Hello? hello?" I called, knowing there would be no doorbell. After a long wait, a young freckle-faced woman came out of the house and walked toward us with a definite, unhurried step. Barefoot, wearing a long black dress almost to the ground, and a kelly-green blouse that complemented her red hair, she looked determined.

"Why are you here?" she asked, brusquely, I thought. The quizzical look on her face seemed to say, "What could these people possibly want?" The look of guarded suspicion remained as I asked her if she would make me a faceless doll.

"Why would you want one?" she asked. "They're so ordinary."

I told her the truth, knowing how odd that explanation must have sounded. "I thought they might teach me something."

"Why do you call them faceless?" she wanted to know.

"All the dolls I'd seen before had their eyes, noses, and mouths drawn in. I call them faceless because the contrast is so startling."

She seemed alternately suspicious and curious, unable to make up her mind. Finally after several minutes, she opened the door and invited us in. Her name was Sarah. Once inside, she was pleased to show us around. To the left was a large kitchen with a black, immaculately polished woodburning stove and a kitchen table with ten chairs around it. To the right was a living room with an old floppy sofa, two straight-back chairs, a small table, bare walls except for a few paper calendars, and a lot of empty space.

Everything in the rooms was sparkling clean.

This was her sister Becky's house, Sarah explained. Becky had nine children, and Sarah, who was not married, lived with her, doing chiropractic work and helping Becky with the children and the garden. "I help Becky catching babies."

"What's that?"

"We're midwives," she said, and went on to explain "We fixed up the two rooms next to the living room with hospital beds so the mothers would be comfortable."

Bursting with curiosity, I blurted out questions. "How do you know when a mother's about to have a baby?" I asked, seeing that as a real problem in a community without telephones.

"They just show up when they're ready. Some come from quite a distance, but we're always around."

"Doesn't a buggy take too long?"

"Oh, some of the women hire drivers to bring them here," Sarah explained matter-of-factly.

After visiting for half an hour I began to feel uneasy taking up Sarah's time. "Will you make a doll for me?" I asked, hoping to have an excuse to stay in contact with her.

"Yes, but I can't tell you exactly when I can send it. I'll have to wait till I have a bit of free time. Is that all right?" She finally agreed to make two dolls for me as long as I understood—I almost had to promise that I understood—they were nothing special.

Then we argued about the price. She said, "Five dollars for each doll."

I said, "You're charging too little." We finally agreed. I would pay fifteen dollars for the two dolls.

Several months later the dolls arrived in a recycled shoe box with a note on lined white paper. I opened the box and saw two serious Amish dolls looking up at me.

The note read, "I hope they are all right. Let me know if you are dissatisfied."

A week later another note arrived, this time from a woman named Ruth, who identified herself as Sarah's cousin. "I hear you like Amish dolls. Would you like me to make you one?" I wrote back, pleased to have an excuse to write to another Amish woman and receive more direct statements on lined white paper.

Over the next six months, I received twelve dolls from seven Amish women.

The dolls surrounded me, silent and serene. I was overcome by the collective energy radiating from them.

Everywhere I looked there was a faceless doll. Some watched while I worked in the studio, a few kept me company upstairs in the room where I saw my clients, two sat on the living room sofa, and several were housed in an old Shaker basket on the dining room table.

Their spirit permeated the house.

They were made by seven ordinary women who spoke no "shoulds."

There was no pecking order there. None was better, none was worse than the others. They didn't have to perform or prove anything. No voice said, "Be happy, cute, or pretty." No voice said, "Be a Star."

In my world everyone has a face, and many of us try to stand out. In their simplicity, these faceless dolls said more with less. They left more to the imagination. Maybe accepting who they are, they don't waste their strength trying to change or compete.

Looking at the dolls, I imagined them worthy companions, friends, allies, and guides for young girls. But were they allowed to cry or be angry, were they itching to be wild and free? Was I talking about myself?

"Tell the truth," they seemed to say. "Don't be afraid. We'll help. Go on! Go on!"

"Where?" I asked. "You'll know! You'll know! Risk. Your heart's desire."

It was hard to admit to myself what I wanted: "To go and live with an Amish family."

Impossible, I told myself. Everyone agreed: no Amish family would take me in. They were religious, hard-working farmers. They didn't reach out to strangers, and they didn't try to proselytize. They chose to live apart from the world and its temptations.

The dolls stood silently by, cheering me on.

CHAPTER THREE

The Journey Begins

In March 1982, a voice in me that didn't make sense said, "Sue, go and live with an Amish family."

I think of myself as a sensible person, not someone who hears voices, or follows them, but this voice sounded so loud and clear and came from such a deep place in me, that it seemed like the voice of a stranger. I had to listen.

"It doesn't make sense," the doubting part of me kept saying. Reasonable, responsible middle-aged women do not hear voices—and they certainly don't follow them. No wonder the sensible part of me panicked. It had taken on a lifetime task of protecting me and felt secure, thinking it had done a good job. Even if protecting me meant keeping me stuck in old patterns, at least they were familiar patterns.

I don't know why, but another part of me trusted the voice. The part that doesn't have to ask a lot of questions or need reasons for doing what it wants to do—it just knows. I knew I had to go.

I told my husband what I planned to do, shouting like a drill sergeant in heavy army boots, declaring my certainty, afraid that if I stopped long enough to take a breath and discuss it reasonably I'd lose my resolve.

I told myself I was going because I was an artist, curious to know more about these farm people who made quilts but never thought of themselves as artists. If my friends had suggested I was setting out on a quest, I would have said they were crazy.

The next day I stared at a map of America, paralyzed. I didn't know where to go. I was drowning in choices: Pennsylvania, Ohio, Iowa, Indiana, Missouri, Illinois, New York, Wisconsin. Which one? I kept hoping an answer would pop out from the map and shout, "Pick me!" That didn't happen.

```
┌─────────────────────────────────────────┐
│              WANTED:                     │
│  Middle-aged married English woman desires │
│  to rent room for a few weeks this summer with │
│       Amish family. She has good habits.  │
│          Contact – Rogers.               │
└─────────────────────────────────────────┘
```

What was my plan? What was the purpose of the trip? I didn't realize that these were the questions I was asking about my life. My growing attraction to the quilts, and even more the mysterious anonymity of the faceless dolls made me nervous. What if they led me off on a path I hadn't planned?

I sent hundreds of letters asking for help. I searched quilting magazines, writing to anyone vaguely connected with Amish life. I even photocopied a picture of my family on the steps of our home in the Berkeley hills—in hopes that people wouldn't be frightened away by my strange request if they saw that I looked normal and was part of a normal-looking family.

I tried everything. I took out a subscription to *Budget*, the Amish weekly newspaper, hoping to find an announcement I could respond to. I wrote to the grandparents of my son's girlfriend, who lived near an Amish community in Iowa, asking if they knew anyone who would take me in. Sensing the urgency of my request, they took out an ad that I read in the May issue of the *Budget*.

Six weeks of silence and not one response. Then, from a woman who had been in my first quilting group, came a picture cut from a newspaper in Iowa. The caption read, "English man, Gerry Smithson, owns an Amish general store in Brimfield, Iowa." A name, a place, and a pleasant face stared back at me from the clipping. I immediately called information and the operator said no such person existed—and with certainty added there was no Amish store in the town.

That evening I went to dinner with two quilt dealers, fine friends, who liked the work I was doing with the Amish squares. They asked how I was, and out poured my frustration.

In an instant everything shifted.

"Oh, Gerry Smithson is a friend of mine," one of the friends said, and picked up the phone.

A few minutes later, I was talking to the owner of the Brimfield General Store, who invited me to stay with him and his wife for a few days. He also warned me not to get my hopes up. "No Amish family will take you in, it's just not done." I was disappointed but also happy to have somewhere to begin.

Two days before I left, I got another call from Gerry. "I found an Amish family for you." Eli Yoder, the minister of the community, thought it was a good idea. I could keep his mother-in-law, Miriam, company. She was a recent widow who was feeling lonely. If it doesn't work out with her, I could stay with Eli, his wife Emma, and their eleven-year-old daughter Lydia. "It will be a good fit," he added.

. . .

I went to the library and came home with a stack of books about the Amish. I wasn't sure I wanted to be told by experts what they were really like. I wanted to keep an open mind, not get bogged down by scholarly facts, but I was curious. Who are these people? Where did they come from? What were their rituals and practices?

The Amish call themselves a "peculiar" people. Was I peculiar for picking them?

They had come to America in the 1720s seeking religious freedom. In Europe, they had been persecuted for their strict beliefs, and their fertile land had been taken away, replaced by barren farm land.

Fearing their influence, the religious and political authorities had decreed that they would not be allowed to own land or live in close-knit communities. When William Penn promised them good land in Pennsylvania and the chance to form their own settlements, they came to America, bringing with them mostly "spiritual baggage."

The Amish are descendants of European Anabaptists, who in the late sixteenth century were the radicals of their day. The Anabaptists, including the followers of Menno Simons called Mennonites, risked their lives trying to change things, believing that earlier Protestants hadn't gone far enough in their reforms. They were named Anabaptists because they were against infant baptism, believing that people should wait till they reached twenty and could make a conscious choice about their religion.

Jacob Ammann, the charismatic Mennonite leader for whom the Amish were named, went even further than other Anabaptists in his demands for strict reform. In the 1690s, he questioned the enormous power and authority of the Catholic church, thinking there should be a clear separation between church and state. He criticized the vanities of the church, the ornate ceremonies, the luxurious clothing worn by priests, believing that something crucial got lost when the hierarchy of the church separated an individual from a direct experience of his God. Religion should be a felt experience. The Amish, his followers, saw themselves as God's chosen people and were taught that God had a personal interest in their lives.

Ammann's beliefs led him to seek a way for his followers to lead a good and decent life. He demanded a return to the *plain and simple.* Pious feelings and simple rural living should go together. He taught them to practice their beliefs. Worshiping in church on Sunday wasn't enough. Applying what they believed day in and day out was what mattered. Customs and traditions reinforced religious beliefs. "By their fruits ye shall know them," the Bible said.

Ammann's quite specific teachings extended into every aspect of daily life. Humility and modesty were valued, and he reinstated some of the earliest Christian rituals—such practices as foot washing—to remind his followers to be humble. He preached nonviolence and told his people to refuse to fight in wars. Ostentation was a sin, a sign of false pride; since buttons were originally used as ornamentation, he insisted that only hooks and eyes be used.

Ammann's intention was to keep the Amish separate and distinct. By remaining apart from the larger community, this "small island of outsiders" would be drawn together. Keeping apart would be the glue that kept them together. He asked for total obedience to an all-knowing God. Obedience was to be tested by how precisely a person followed the rules. Those who broke the rules were disciplined zealously. Excommunication wasn't a harsh enough punishment, so Ammann initiated a practice called "shunning." Anyone who strayed from the rules might not be allowed to eat with the family, do business with neighbors, or even sleep with his or her mate. The entire fabric of an ordered life could be shattered if an individual broke the rules.

Horrified by what I had read, I closed the books. I hate being told what to do and not to do. I had loved it when my young son made a birthday card, calling me *Free Bender*.

But the people who I was about to visit, who made the quilts I loved, spent their lives following rules.

CHAPTER FOUR

Testing the Dream

Several months later, in June, a friend who was about to drive cross-country, agreed to drop me off at my destination, Brimfield, Iowa. As we approached the town, life shifted gears. Suddenly, there were no more suburbs or factories, no more 7-Elevens, McDonald's, gas stations, or billboards. But most of all, there was no clutter.

We followed the signs to the Brimfield General Store. Like most Amish buildings, it was a modest wooden structure, white with black trim. It stood alone just off the road, surrounded on both sides by a vast green pasture. Three black buggies, their horses hitched in the shade at the side of the building, were parked at the front porch.

My friend parked the car next to the buggies, and we walked into the small, uncluttered store. It contained everything. Old, carefully preserved wood-paneled countertops and display cases held carpentry supplies, material for clothing and quilting, food staples, candy, stationery, shoes, seed, household cleaning supplies, and a freezer for ice cream.

We were greeted by a man in his sixties with remarkable, sparkling eyes, a brilliant green shirt, bushy whiskers, and a welcoming grin stretching from ear to ear. This was Levi, Gerry Smithson's right-hand man, and the manager of the Brimfield General Store. He offered us some peanuts and said Gerry and his wife, Essie, would be back shortly.

I felt self-conscious. I didn't belong.

It was a warm June afternoon. Wearing a beige, short-sleeved cotton shirt and grey cotton skirt, I felt naked. Everyone else who came into the store was wearing simple, yet heavy farmers' clothing reminiscent of the eighteenth century. Suddenly, eating our peanuts, trying not to stand out as we watched each new customer enter the store, my friend and I were the peculiar ones.

Three men were having a lively conversation at a small wooden table near the front of the store. Two six-year-olds came in and ordered ice cream cones, several women purchased food supplies, and one woman picked out three yards of material for a dress. Two teenagers helped Levi take care of the customers.

My first impression was that they all looked alike. Alike and austere.

The females—little girls, young mothers, old women—all looked the same: hair parted in the middle, drawn tightly back from the face, wrapped in a bun, and covered with a black bonnet. They wore long dresses, almost touching the floor, in dark solid brown, grey, and navy blue. Their dresses had high necks and long sleeves and were covered by dark, contrasting aprons, almost as long as the dresses, that crossed over their shoulders and were pinned in the front. Their practical black shoes were the kind nuns wore.

In keeping with Ammann's teaching of *plain and simple*, the men wore their hair uncut—shoulder length—and their beards untrimmed—full and bushy like William Penn's. Their trousers were cut wide and full in heavy fabric. Some wore suspenders, but no one wore a belt.

There was something unsettling about their quiet sameness, the holding-back way they carried themselves, almost merging with their surroundings. It was as if everyone had conferred beforehand

and agreed that no one would stand out.

I liked to stand out. Usually I wore distinctive old Arabic and pre-Colombian jewelry and liked people to ask me where it came from. I had decided to leave my jewelry at home, but in this setting I stood out without even wanting to. I was good at spotting the extrovert, the shy one, the person who was just trying a little too hard to impress, but here those skills were useless.

But when I looked again, I saw that their clothing wasn't all drab. Touches of bright purple, electric green, vibrant blue showed in their blouses and shirts. The intense color created a dramatic contrast in the midst of all the plainness.

Later I noticed that underneath their almost floor-length dresses, Ida and Sadie, the two Amish teenagers helping out at the store, were wearing flashy electric blue running shoes with lightning bolts on the sides. What rule allowed running shoes?

My friend left me that afternoon, and I joined Gerry and Essie Smithson in their home behind the Brimfield General Store. The following morning I sat under a giant oak tree next to the store, looked out at the peaceful landscape and cried. I was exhausted, excited, and afraid.

I had made an impossible dream real. I had said "Yes, I want," and here I was. The old quilts and the faceless dolls had led me this far, but why I was here, what I was really looking for, or hoping to find, was not at all clear. Instead, I worried if I would be able to settle down in this quiet land.

. . .

The next day, I met the Yoders.

Gerry drove me over to meet them, and I got out of his car and stood facing the simple Amish farmhouse. A windmill not far from the house turned slowly in the slight breeze and cast its shadow over a red barn with acres of farm land beyond it. Then I saw Emma Yoder, heavy set with a round, kindly face, and Lydia, her gangly eleven-year-old daughter, coming out, smiling, to greet me. I felt like Margaret O'Brien in an old movie—a waif, suitcase in hand and courage in her heart, awaiting her fate.

I said good-bye to Gerry and followed Emma and Lydia through a side door into the house. We went through a utility room and came into the large sunny kitchen, with its central table, black-metal woodburning stove, a linoleum floor and speckled beige Formica counters, something like the ones I had at home—nothing distinctive, neither old-fashioned nor modern.

But the room glowed.

The feeling went beyond everyday cleanliness and order. The air felt alive, almost vibrating. Can a room have a heartbeat? Can space be serene and exciting at the same time? I'd never been in a room that felt like that.

I usually walked around in an excited state, my mind racing, but after being in the kitchen for a few minutes, I slowed down and began to feel calm. The difference was so dramatic that I wondered if this was what an altered state of consciousness was like.

Emma asked if I'd like a cup of coffee, and she fixed Nescafé and brought out some delicious chocolate chip cookies she had just baked.

"Would you like to meet my father?" Lydia asked, after chatting for a few minutes. "He's down the road helping a neighbor." Walking along a country road with this lively preteen Amish girl, I was surprised how comfortable she was with me. I thought of my own children and their friends, who were often ill at ease talking with grown-ups. This supposedly unworldly young person, cut off from television, newspapers, movies, and radio, carried on a lively and intelligent conversation. When we got to the barn where her father was stacking bales of hay, she introduced us.

Eli, who was slim and wiry, looked at me through thin, metal-rimmed glasses. Like Levi, the manager of the general store, he had a twinkle in his eye. After meeting his chubby wife, I thought he looked as if he had come from a more modern generation that knew being fat wasn't healthy.

"I'm a little out of breath," he said. "I work hard all day, and then I do this." He wasn't apologizing or bragging, just saying what was on his mind. "We'd better get all that hay in the barn before the rains come," he explained. I thought he was quite charming and full of fun.

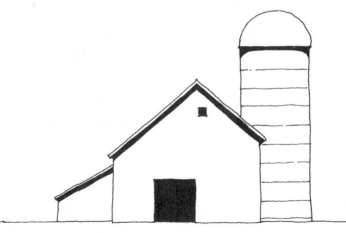

On the way home, Lydia described her father's routine. Besides working thirteen hours a day as a farmer and blacksmith, Eli was the minister for his community, a job he would hold for life, with no pay yet great responsibility. His day started at 5 A.M., feeding the animals, then off to work at the blacksmith shop several miles away. Lydia enjoyed her new role as my teacher, and I felt lucky to have such an enthusiastic guide to introduce me to the ways of her world.

Lydia pointed to a wizened old woman with a small wrinkled face stepping down from a horse-drawn carriage to take the harness off her horse. "There's my grandma Miriam," Lydia said as we walked toward her.

Lifting the harness, which looked as though it weighed more than she did, was an amazing feat for a tiny old woman. "It's man's work, but I have to do it," Miriam said as she greeted us. The statement was neither a complaint nor an apology; she was just letting me know what was so. I helped her carry the groceries into her house. She started the motor for the water pump, then eagerly showed me her garden. "My daughter Emma produces more than enough in her garden. I could use her vegetables, but I want to be independent," she told me.

As Lydia and I walked back along the path that joined her house to the small house in which her grandmother lived, she explained, "My grandmother and grandfather used to live in our big house, but now my parents run the farm, so they built a small house next door for their parents. It's our tradition—we switch houses when our parents get older. We call it the grossdadi house."

Miriam joined us for dinner that first night. "I usually eat at my home, but tonight's special," she explained. Eli acted as the host, surrounded by his harem: wife, daughter, mother-in-law, and now me. He did most of the talking, asking me questions about my life in California. Emma, by contrast, was quiet and shy, almost disappearing into the background.

"It's courageous of you to take me in," I said.

"Yes," Eli said, "but I don't think there will be any lawsuits."

"Emma, you're a good cook," I said, trying to turn the conversation around to include her. "Yes, and she looks it," Eli added, looking at his round wife, before she had a chance to answer.

After dinner I asked if I could do the dishes. Emma was hesitant. "Bet you have a dishwasher at home," she said tentatively. "Bet you have two," Eli added quickly before I had a chance to answer. I felt uncomfortable. Did I have to apologize for having a dishwasher? I looked at each person at the table, wondering what they thought of me, what each one's fantasy was of my life in California. What made them decide to take me in? Was it Eli's idea, and the women had agreed to go along?

Lydia was given the task of showing me the dishwashing routine. She was specific and definite, and I understood immediately that I would have to pay attention and follow her instructions exactly. The plastic dishes were first rinsed in one container, washed, and then' rinsed again in another container to save water. Then each dish was dried and put away. Each step was done with complete attention—a cup placed here, a dish lined up there, nothing random. Simple movements, simple activities, all adding up to an unspoken ritual they all understood and followed.

I smiled as I thought about how I did the dishes—a small symbol of the pride I took in thinking of myself as a free spirit. Dishes were high on my list of hateful chores. If I was in the midst of cleaning up and got an idea for work in the studio, I dropped everything and left the dishes half-done. Creative people could be disorderly and undisciplined, I told myself—and besides, that much routine and certainty would be boring.

After I did the dishes, Emma showed me to my upstairs bedroom. It was Lydia's room, and she had happily moved downstairs to the room next to her parents that she had as a child. My room, which faced the road, was comfortable and nondescript, with a double bed, large closet, and a few souvenirs Lydia had collected. Emma, carrying a bucket of store-bought vanilla ice cream under her arm, said goodnight, letting me know they were off in the buggy to their neighbors' house to celebrate a birthday.

When they were gone, Miriam asked if I'd like to come over to her house and visit for a while. "I was afraid someone who didn't know our ways wouldn't know how to use the kerosene stove," she said.

"And there've been a lot of fires lately from those stoves. That's why I changed my mind about your staying with me."

We talked by the soft light of a flickering kerosene lamp, and she told me about her weekly routine. Three times a week she and her sister did housecleaning for English families. Her sister was a Mennonite now, a sect not as strict as the Amish. "She's allowed to drive a car."

"Are you allowed to ride in a car?" I asked, thinking it might be against her religious beliefs.

"Oh, it's fine, we just can't own one. We drive to town and it gives me something to do. I like keeping busy and I like doing the work and I like the extra spending money. Oh, we really scrub the walls down and get the floors sparkling. Some of those English houses sure are messy." I could tell by the sound of her voice that she enjoyed the work and the excuse to ride in a car. Listening to the delight in her voice when she talked about housecleaning made me wish I could take her home to help me clean my house. Housework, like doing dishes, was low on my list of satisfying work.

"Some evenings when I get home tired, I sure wish I could just turn on an electric light," she continued. Then, thinking I might misunderstand, she reassured me and perhaps herself. "I wouldn't really want to change. We Amish want to stay the way we are."

After saying goodnight, I walked back to Eli and Emma's, listening to a silence that was broken only by the occasional clumpity-clump of horses' hooves on the road, my mind flooded with impressions. Then, tired and happy, I crawled into a lumpy bed and fell asleep.

At five the next morning we knelt in the living room to say the morning prayer. "Thank you, God, for all your help, forgive us our sins, help us with the land," Eli said. In my honor they said the prayer in English. They spoke a German dialect with each other, but could easily switch back and forth. After the prayer, Eli and Lydia went out to feed the four horses, two cows, one goat, and innumerable chickens. Then the animals were put out to pasture. Emma gathered eggs. Then we sat down to breakfast.

To my horror, breakfast consisted of sugared cereal with a dollop of honey and a few teaspoons of sugar added for good measure, store-bought white bread and butter, sweet homemade jam, and Sanka with five teaspoons of sugar.

I was living in white-sugar heaven. I mostly watched and nibbled on white bread toast, not ready to give up my regime of freshly squeezed orange juice, granola, whole wheat bread, and nonfat milk.

By six, Eli was off in his buggy. After he left, Emma, Miriam, Lydia, and I went to the garden. We picked buckets and buckets of peas and then hauled them into the kitchen. Out came huge stainless steel pots that still looked new, even though Emma said she'd had them for twenty-five years. It was the same with the

shining black cast-iron woodburning stove, which turned out to be thirty years old. "We're just five or six people. Why do we need such gigantic pots?" I asked. "They could feed an army."

"We'll cook some for dinner, but we'll can the rest," Emma said. "That way we'll be prepared."

"Sometimes our whole family gets together and that can be two hundred people," she said. "We try to be self-sufficient." They willingly spend time preparing and preserving food. Most of the summer harvest would be set aside for winter eating. Without freezers there was lots of pickling—in the basement I saw cabinets filled with tomato relish, three kinds of bean salad, and cole slaw. Quantities were impressive—forty-six quarts of applesauce, ninety pounds of chicken, and forty of hamburger. Seeing my astonishment, Lydia added, "Last week we were very busy canning sixty-four jars of tomatoes. We made at least four bushels of them ready for ketchup. Then we cut up the tomatoes and put them in big white buckets with salt and let them stand about a week. Every day we dumped off excess water that came to the top. After a week we put them in kettles and cook them down to the right thickening, and add spices and sugar."

"The less we have to buy at the market, the better," Emma added.

That day we sterilized large glass jars, boiled the peas, and canned them, working steadily, chatting as we went along at an even rhythm, allowing the work to get done, task by task, an unfolding process. I watched each of them—marveling at their ability to be relaxed as they worked and to stay focused on one thing at a time. When we finished, we had forty jars of peas, each labeled and dated, to place in neat rows in the cellar.

No one rushed.

Each step was done with care.

The women moved through the day unhurried. There was no rushing to finish so they could get on to the "important things." For them, it was all important.

Perhaps they had inherited the same routine from their mothers and grandmothers. It was clear someone had spent time thinking and planning how to do each task in the most useful and efficient way. Now it was automatic, the repetition ingrained, no time had to be wasted questioning how it should be done—they worked relaxed, "unconsciously conscious." "We grew up learning to sew, cook, quilt, can, and garden," Emma said, "hardly realizing when it happened."

Which parts of today's process were a chore? Which were fun? There seemed to be no separation for them.

Time was full and generous. It was as if they had uncovered a way to be in time, to be a part of time, to have a harmonious relation with time.

For me time was a burden.

There was never enough of it. In Berkeley I ran around breathlessly rushing toward impossible goals—and to that vague "something out there." When I explained how split I was, loving to do certain things and hating to do others, the women laughed and tried to understand.

"Making a batch of vegetable soup, it's not right for the carrot to say I taste better than the peas, or the pea to say I taste better than the cabbage. It takes all the vegetables to make a good soup!" Miriam said.

Miriam's sharp sense of humor kept us entertained. As we worked, she told funny stories about her childhood.

As the days passed, I felt I was living in a still-life painting. In the background was a soft, sweeping farm landscape, and in the foreground were many people, all busy doing their chores with silent grace.

Everything was a ritual.

Doing the dishes, mowing the lawn, baking bread, quilting, canning, hanging out the laundry, picking fresh produce, weeding. Friday: housecleaning; Saturday: mowing the lawn; Monday: washing. Emma, Lydia, and Miriam, three generations of women living side by side, knew exactly what had to be done and in what order. Nothing had to be explained.

No distinction was made between the sacred and the everyday.

Five minutes in the early morning and five minutes in the evening were devoted to prayer. The rest of the day was spent living their beliefs. Their life was all one piece. It was all sacred—and all ordinary.

They practiced daily what they believed. They never preached to me. They never said, "Our way is better." Deeds, not words, mattered. How they lived reflected their faith.

Everyone drew from the same text, the Bible. They knew who they were by the stories they told, the same themes, repeated over and over. The Bible not only told them who they were but explained the world and their relation to it. In every home I saw a copy of the *Book of Martyrs*, which reminded them of their ancestors' sacrifice for what they believed.

They had inherited a set of obligations, which helped define who they were and where they fit into the larger whole. A set of practices provided a context for morality and made it clear how a good person ought to be. With that came a clear understanding of the moral relations between people, which became part of the fabric of their lives.

I was happy pitching in and feeling useful, but I hadn't learned how to relax and just be with the family. I wanted to do an art project, something that would be uniquely mine. I decided to make something connected to the Amish squares, but I needed cotton and all I saw around me was polyester. For an Amish mother with twelve children, polyester was a godsend. It meant no ironing. The women shook their heads when they saw me in my wrinkled cotton and linen clothing, thinking me old-fashioned. They also probably thought me foolish for choosing the cotton, but they never would have said that out loud.

I asked several neighbors if they had any old clothing I could use for a project. But they didn't know or trust me yet, so they said no. Even Miriam said no. I decided to walk to a town ten miles away, to find Zook's Department Store, famous for its vast supply of solid-colored cotton fabrics.

I had decided not to rent a car, afraid that I'd be tempted to do too many things, and walking might be more in keeping with the rhythm of their daily life.

No one "took a walk" in Brimfield. They laughed and thought it funny when I described walking as an exercise regime. Exercise wasn't a separate activity. Walking barefoot, running barefoot, whatever the chore, they were in it, of it, doing it with a sturdy grace—very much connected to the ground.

Now, as I walked across their countryside, the Amish stared. I was the "peculiar" one. Families in buggies nodded, giving a half-wave, acknowledging some relationship. Without a telephone, everyone knew everyone else's business. By now the word was out—the Yoders had taken in a stranger from California.

"Am I on the right road?" I kept asking, unsure of my destination, literally, figuratively, on every level.

On this hot summer day, the walk seemed to take forever. Buggy rides were offered, but my determination to walk won out. Zook's Department Store was my reward. Bolt after bolt, row after row of splendid cotton colors. "It's no bother," they assured me, as they cut a one-eighth-yard piece from each of the twenty-five bolts I'd selected. With a ten-dollar bundle under my arm and some shoofly pie in my belly, I headed home.

. . .

"Would it be all right to work on the kitchen floor?" I felt brazen asking and didn't want to intrude on their routine, but my room had no extra floor space and poor light. I remember Margaret Mead saying that anthropologists have a choice: they can either enter the family system of the tribe as a brother or sister and live by their rules, or remain outside the system, observing them and asking questions. I wanted to join in, but I also wanted to ask questions. Of course, I wasn't there as an anthropologist, psychologist, or sociologist. I still wasn't sure why I was there.

"Can I help?" Lydia asked as she saw me begin to cut out a pile of one-inch squares to make groups of ninepatches.

"Of course."

I measured and she began to cut. Titus, her twelve-year-old cousin who had come over to help Eli with the chores, shyly asked if he could join in. "Of course."

As a designer, I am quite definite. I have strong opinions and don't care if others agree or not, but now as the three of us worked, I asked Lydia and Titus if they wanted to design the project. That sounds easy enough, but letting someone else take charge was a big step for me. "You don't have to be in charge all the time," I had to reassure myself.

Lydia and Titus plunged in, choosing from the pile of colors. They worked separately, moving the squares around, arranging and re-arranging. What emerged was a remarkable array of highly original color combinations, variations on the ninepatch pattern. Lydia's eye was especially good. Where did she learn this?

"Maybe I can find some old dresses," Miriam offered, after watching the flurry of excitement. "I can't use them for anything else, so if you like, we can cut them up." Hearing her say "we" sounded lovely. No longer suspicious, she returned with a bundle of old and very worn dresses. I had passed an unspoken test, and now her old clothes, a part of her history, could join my new patches.

Emma looked on, enjoying the pleasure the children were having and especially my appreciation for Lydia's newfound talent. "Maybe I could sew them up for you on my machine," she said hesitantly. She had an old-fashioned treadle sewing machine.

To me, sewing the fragments had always made them feel contained and hemmed in, but I didn't want to interfere with the process. At that moment, Emma's wanting to be a part of what was happening was more important than my artistic prejudices. She stitched the pieces together and delighted in watching the nine-patches take shape.

Next it was Miriam's turn to offer her services. Decisions had to be made about size and proportions, and the relationship of the inner and outer border. To be old is to be respected in this community, and Miriam, the senior member of our team, was clearly in charge. She knew the rules—and the rules were to be followed. "I'll put it on a frame and quilt it, " she said.

Our collaboration grew.

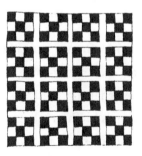

By noon, the immaculate kitchen was a mess. I couldn't believe what I was seeing. I had turned their pristine, orderly household into a three-ring circus. What would happen if Eli came home for lunch and saw this? Timid Emma assured me it would be all right.

We had traded roles. For the moment, I was more of an Amish wife than Emma, worried what my "husband" might think and unwilling to risk finding out. I gathered up the hundreds of extra pieces we had created and carried them upstairs before Eli arrived.

The Amish don't want people to photograph them, but we had produced a "photograph" more vivid than any camera could have taken. This eighteen-by-twenty-two-inch ninepatch quilt, "Lydia's Square," hangs in my studio, a happy reminder of that day.

■   ■   ■

Though the Yoder family delighted in being frugal, I noticed pockets of excess.

One evening I came home from a quilting bee—where twelve women, ages twenty-two to eighty-five, had sat around a large quilting frame, working, chatting, and gossiping—to find seven women gathered at Emma's kitchen table. A party was underway, and Emma brought out her plastic trays, twenty of them, each with five partitions. My job was to heap massive amounts of popcorn, pretzels, corn puffs, cake, ice cream, and syrups into the trays. "Sue, you give such small portions," one woman chided me, but the women's portions looked gargantuan. A serving of ice cream was five scoops, and many of the guests asked for seconds.

The men sat in the living room, enjoying the friendship of their neighbors. The younger children frisked outside, while the teenagers gathered by the barn, talking quietly. When everyone had eaten, the women cleared the plates and washed the dishes. Then everyone, old and young, converged on the living room. They all knew what to do, and without instruction opened their prayer books and began to sing.

Out poured glorious, robust four-part harmony, sung in rounds. The sound filled the entire house. The Yoders had started their day with a prayer for the land, worked hard, and then good friends and family came together to end their day with joyous singing.

The Yoders weren't poor, but their diet was awful: a Swiss-German farmer's preference for dumplings, butter and cream, jams, and sugary desserts. Out in the garden were fresh vegetables. I longed for salad but got lettuce and white bread sandwiches with mayonnaise. "Pass the fat, pass the carbohydrates," I imagined them saying. Each day we picked sweet, fresh strawberries, but before they reached the table, they'd been sabotaged by mounds of sugar.

I was a prisoner of the sweet-tooth fairy. Emma thought I was teasing when I said that my husband and I didn't use a pound of sugar in a year. She bought sugar in fifteen-pound sacks, several times a year.

I wanted to be a good guest, but finally I had to say something. I told them about salads. "You're so slim, Sue, maybe it would be a good idea for me to eat salad," Emma said. I went into the garden and picked fresh lettuce, then improvised a dressing. They stared at what I had made. Later, Lydia told me they never eat tomatoes "raw"—they peel the skins, and "plain" lettuce was just too strange.

* * *

"The ladies are going for a toot," Eli announced one morning, "and they'd like to take you along." It had all been arranged: Frieda, a Mennonite, would take us in her car. Though they weren't allowed to drive or own a car, the Amish women were delighted to go on this expedition. I wondered if they were disappointed that I hadn't come in a car. Eli said they weren't against talking on the telephone, but acquiring possessions might lead to temptation, and they didn't want to become dependent on the outside world.

The women had various errands: going first to a store famous for good-quality clothing and sturdy material, and then to a drugstore that sold expensive vitamins. I was surprised to see them buying deodorant, mouthwash, aloe vera skin lotions—a lot of items I labeled nonessential. Lydia asked for a particularly ugly plastic doll.

In their world they chose well, but when faced with a bewildering array of choices in the outside community, they often chose unwisely. In fact, before the 1850s, when they led a spartan and isolated life, their homes were bare, but handsome. Now with affluence, many homes had fussy china proudly displayed in living room cupboards.

The highlight of our trip was a stop at the *Essenhaus,* where each woman already knew from past visits what to order: fried mush with maple syrup for one; slices of apple, boysenberry, and cherry pie for another; I chose gravy and stuffing. Then Frieda drove us home, each of us paying her four dollars for the "toot."

That evening Eli announced, "We're going to a cattle auction to-night." It was his turn for an outing. The Amish loved going to auctions. Recycling household goods, farm machinery, or animals appealed to their practical nature. After a long day's work, a cattle auction was a chance to visit with friends and learn the latest cattle prices. Eli was thinking of selling Otto, the youngest of his buggy horses. Otto didn't want to take orders, and that proved dangerous in traffic.

It was my first buggy ride. Lydia and I huddled together in the back seat with a blanket over our laps, while Emma and Eli sat in the front. How restful the ride was, no rushing to pass another buggy or beat out a red light. Instead of a clock, Eli had a calendar on his dashboard. The hour it took to go five miles was slow enough to savor the landscape and still arrive on time.

As soon as we arrived, Eli hurried to join a group of men engrossed in lively conversation. Emma looked stranded. "Shall we go and join them?" I suggested.

"Oh, no, I can't do that," Emma answered, horrified by my suggestion. "That wouldn't be proper."

"Why isn't that proper?"

"One of the men is my cousin, but I don't know the others," Emma said. There was no use arguing with her. We walked by ourselves, Emma nodding to an occasional woman.

During the auction, Eli and his next-door neighbor, Ervin, delighted in teaching me, the ignorant city person, about the kinds of cattle being sold, what to look for, and why some brought much higher prices than others. Although I felt disloyal to Emma, I loved being with them.

The buggy ride home was magic, the sky lit by thousands of fireflies.

Eli interrupted my reverie. "Did you know that Kenny Bucholtzer, our neighbor, was hit by a speeding car on this road last week?"

. . .

There wasn't much need for Doctor Spock in this community. "If a baby cries," Emma said, "there is always a good reason." If I had been given a choice, I would have wanted to spend the first two years of my life in an Amish household, two blissful years of being accepted and adored and considered entirely blameless.

"After two years of that kind of loving support, isn't it harsh to switch?" I asked Eli, knowing that at two a child starts to be taught obedience and conformity.

"Our way is fair and consistent," Eli answered. "At two, children are ready to learn. We don't believe that some children are born saved, and others are sinners. Sin only comes when you know the difference between good and evil, and a baby doesn't know, so it can't sin. All children are born with sin, through no fault of their own, and all children can be taught to live the good way."

Babies are included in all aspects of family life. As soon as they are able, children are given chores and quickly learn that they have a useful role in the family. The whole community pitches in to teach children respect for its values.

A child learns from a very early age the value of work—that work is enjoyable, important, and should be respected. The Amish find meaning in work itself. Work is never viewed as a stepping stone to personal success or advancement but a challenge to do whatever you are doing to the best of your ability.

I thought sibling rivalry was normal, but as I watched children play with their younger brothers, sisters, and cousins and looked for signs of furtive pinches, jealousy, and competition, I didn't see any. They weren't saints, but baby-sitting was fun.

The Amish leave school after the eighth grade because they fear further learning might lead a person off the path of humility and toward a feeling of self-importance. Even so, every person I met spoke two languages, switching back and forth with ease, and understood a high German that was used in the Sunday service, while I, with two master's degrees, remained mute in every foreign land I ever visited.

·   ·   ·

"Why is the Amish land so beautiful?" I asked one evening. "What makes it feel special? I'm a city person, Eli, and I didn't see a cow till I was twelve. I don't know where the sun sets, or how to tell which way the wind blows, or distinguish one crop from another, but I have eyes, and I trust my heart. This land is loved."

"The land is God's," Eli said. "It's my job, and the job of every Amish person to take care of it for Him. We mustn't try to change or conquer nature or exploit the land. That would be going against God's way."

When Eli talked about the land, he was happy.

I saw him work hard and saw the glorious results of that work. Wasn't that changing nature? Eli said he couldn't tell me what English farmers did, but he could tell me something about his way with the land.

"Caring for the land, every day, is my way to be close to God. His land must be honored," Eli said, and he tried to feel close to God while he worked. As he talked, I saw the land as a living thing. I could feel his relationship with God and the land expressed daily, in an infinite number of ways.

The Amish make a lifetime commitment to their land, and their religious beliefs even determine farming methods. Over the years they have learned that with patience and perseverence they can transform dry, harsh land into a workable field. They have devised innovative ways to improve God's land without power equipment: the rotation of crops, the use of irrigation and natural fertilizers, and the planting of alfalfa and clover all help to revitalize the land.

Most Amish farmers own less than one hundred acres, keeping their farms small so horses can be used instead of tractors and neighbors can pitch in with the chores. In this way the community remains an intimate, manageable size. "Brotherly love" becomes an economic asset.

Their intention is to make things grow and do work that is useful. I couldn't say exactly what the difference is, but I felt a difference. They work to work. Their work time isn't spent "in order to do something else"—to have free time on weekends, go to a restaurant, or save for a vacation or retirement. They do not expect to find satisfaction in that vague "something out there" but in the daily mastery of whatever they are doing.

The Amish strive to create an ecology of no waste; the land supplies food for the family and the animals, and the family and the animals do the work. "Manure is our crucial crop," Eli joked. "Tractors don't make manure!" A horse reproduces itself, he explained, and a tractor only makes debts.

. . .

The lives of the Amish are ordered by the seasons. Weddings are held in November and December, when the harvest is finished. While the land rests, the women quilt and sew, waiting for spring and the land's next active cycle.

The inherent order that permeated their lives began to calm me.

The order I saw in their clothesline puts them in touch with the order of life. The black buggy came from the same world as the simple white house with the black trim.

Because their way of dressing was so different than mine, I was struck by how similiar they looked to one another. But they could determine in an instant where someone belonged in their structured society. Dozens of different brim sizes on men's hats disclosed the wearer's age and marital status. If men wore one or two shoulder straps and if the straps were crossed or not gave information about their church group. Men shaved until they married and then grew beards. From age twelve until marriage, girls wore black hats with their Sunday dresses and white hats at home.

Delicate, small embroidery at the cuffs of otherwise unadorned sleeves means a girl in her late teens is ready to study for baptism. It's also the time for her to join other teenagers at a Sunday "singing"—the place where the communities' courting ritual begins.

They knew where they belonged, and in hundreds of different ways they let each other know who they were and where they fit in their universe.

■ ■ ■

On Sunday, there was no work. *No Sunday Sales* signs appeared everywhere. Everything stopped. A new vibration was in the air, a quiet excitement. Emma scurried around the house, making sure that everyone's clothes were just right, checking that Lydia's Sunday bonnet had all its pleats lined up, that her apron and shawl fit properly. Finally, after all that busyness, they emerged, transformed, sparkling in their Sunday finery.

Eli traded his overalls for a handsome suit that was beautifully cut from expensive, dark grey worsted material. He looked dignified and elegant, more like someone who had just come from his tailor than a hardworking Amish farmer from Iowa.

"How did you get to be the minister?" I asked Eli. "Oh, it was nothing," he shrugged. "I was hit by lot." He outlined the procedure for me. All the full-fledged members of the church, men and women, gathered in someone's house and walked in single file past a door or an open window, each whispering the name of someone they thought was qualified for the job. The deacon stood on the other side of the door or window and listened.

Those nominated had to meet two qualifications. They had to be married and good at managing their farms. I didn't need to ask if a woman could be a minister.

The deacon wrote down the name of anyone who received two votes, three votes in some communities. If five qualified candidates were chosen, five hymn books were placed on the table. The deacon hid a piece of paper in one of the books and the person who picked that book would become the new minister. "He's 'hit by lot,' " Eli said. "That way, it's the choice of God."

This practice left no room for self-importance. Once chosen, the minister became leader with enormous responsibility, but instead of congratulating him, most of their friends felt sorry for Eli, and for Emma.

"Why do you have the service in your homes?" I asked.

"We're Old Order Amish, and we believe in keeping things simple," Eli answered. They took turns hosting the service and designed their houses with wide doors and movable partitions. On Sunday, they bring in long folding benches from a special wagon made just to carry and store them.

"How many people belong to your church?"

"About twenty to thirty families. That's about how many can fit into one house, and it's still few enough for everyone to know each other's name. That's important to us." Eli spoke of families, not individuals. When I asked how many people that was, he seemed surprised by my question, and had to spend several minutes thinking about the answer. It was as hard for me, who lived in a *see me* world, to think in terms of a group as it was for Eli to think in terms of individuals. "It's about two hundred people," he finally said.

"Why are you baptized as young adults?" I asked Eli.

"That way you have time to think about such an important decision, one that will affect the rest of your life."

This was a coming of age ritual, a rite of passage. Once a young person chose to be baptized, everything changed.

As if to emphasize the importance of the decision, more freedom was given to teenagers. I heard that many boys ran wild—drinking, smoking, and even owning cars, which seemed inconsistent with their strict upbringing. The girls also had more freedom, but the boys especially could "run around," as they called it, and face the temptations of the outside world. Worried parents looked the other way and hoped that with patience the seeds of family loyalty and group harmony they had planted would grow.

This was the time for the teenagers to make a choice. That was what it was about. Making a conscious choice. Becoming an adult member of this community meant "act responsibly." That's when Ida and Sadie, the teenaged sales clerks in Brimfield, would have to trade in their glorious blue running shoes, the ones with the lightning bolt, for a pair of black shoes.

When did I become an adult? I wondered.

I might have argued that the purpose of their early training was to indoctrinate them to make that crucial choice. Almost every large family had someone who left to join an "easier" church. Easier means a church with fewer restrictions. Yet, even with people leaving—and about twenty percent do leave—the number who choose to stay continues to grow, and the membership of the Old Order Amish is increasing.

I was relieved and disappointed not to be invited to church—the only one left at home. "Sunday's the only day we lock our doors," Eli called out as they stepped into the buggy and waved good-bye.

• • •

It was easy to be romantic about their communal sharing. The Amish way was full of connections, and mine was equally full of disconnections.

I wondered and worried about those individuals who broke the community's rules. How could the gentle people I cared about practice shunning—the complete ostracism of a person from all social contact?

I never saw an example of shunning directly and never heard it discussed. Was it a family secret, a community secret? Was it something they took for granted and didn't have to think about?

I didn't have the courage to ask them directly. I was afraid they would hear the horrified judgment in my voice.

What most disturbed me was that the accused couldn't defend themselves against the charges. If they "confessed fault" and prom-

ised to change, they might be reinstated into the good graces of the community. Their other choices were to remain as outcasts or move away. News of their crimes would follow them to other Amish groups, and they'd have difficulty being welcomed into a new community.

For me it still seemed all or nothing. If you followed the rules, you belonged and reaped the benefits of a close-knit community. If you broke the rules, "you were on ice at home and in hot water in the community." If I had been able to talk to Eli about shunning, I could imagine him saying, "Standards must be met. If you care about your community, then commitment to the rules is important. Otherwise we'd disappear and just melt into the English world that surrounds us." For him it would be a crime not to support his principles.

■　■　■

Eli refused to put up lightning rods to protect his home and barn from disaster. "You work hard, why won't you protect yourself?"

"That would be interfering with God's direction," he said, wondering why I was making such a fuss. When he told me he had no property or life insurance, I was really concerned.

"What happens when a disaster comes?"

"Everyone comes to the rescue," he smiled, making it sound simple. I must have had a strange look on my face, for he added,

"You seem so worried. Really, there's nothing unusual about it—we just pitch in. Nothing special about that."

Miriam had said much the same thing a few days earlier. Amos, Emma's fourteen-year-old nephew who had been hit by a car, was in a Chicago hospital. While Amos's mother went to visit him, Emma helped with the housekeeping, and Eli helped out in the fields. When I told Miriam I thought that was very generous, she sounded surprised, "Oh, no, it's nothing, really. It's just our way."

Caring for other members of the community was taken for granted. Retarded and sick people were not only cared for but thought of as a gift of God, an opportunity to express brotherly love.

I knew the Amish refused to accept Social Security and medical benefits, fearing they would become dependent on the outside community. How could Amos's family afford his staggering hospital bills? "Oh, the Amish Aid Society takes care of that. We take care of our own," Miriam told me.

"How do you raise the money?"

"We give as much as we can."

These neighbors and friends had a kind of security I didn't have. In times of sickness, accidents, financial setbacks, or natural disasters, they know support will be there. Miriam, who was seventy-eight and had sixty-three grandchildren, expected her children would want to take care of her as she got older, and it was hard for her to imagine that not happening.

Brotherly love was their insurance.

Who is richer? I wondered. How rich and varied my life was in some ways, and how poor and disconnected it was in others. "Let's pool our equipment," I had suggested to a friendly neighbor when I first moved into my home in Berkeley. She thought that was a great idea and for the next two years I borrowed her Electrolux vacuum and for two years she borrowed nothing. The third year I bought my own Electrolux.

In keeping with the simplicity of their lives, when someone died, family members made a basic pine box coffin. White was never used in quilts but was saved for funerals. At the service the minister would deliver a short eulogy that showed respect but offered no extravagant praise.

■　■　■

Hoping to reciprocate in a small way for their hospitality, I asked if I could invite the Yoders to a restaurant. "No, it's not necessary," they insisted, but they finally agreed and were excited at the prospect of a new adventure. Would they like to try something they'd never tasted—Chinese, Italian, or Mexican? They plunged in, exploring the possibilities. Although they couldn't pick up the phone to ask a neighbor or check the food critics' latest report, they had their "network," which led us to the basement of a Mexican church.

Frieda and Jacob, their Mennonite neighbors, would join Emma, Eli, Lydia, Miriam, and me for the celebration. All of us happily squeezed into Frieda and Jacob's two cars.

The combination special—taco, enchilada, and burrito, complete for $2.35—was everyone's choice. Gleefully we cleaned our plates.

As long as it fit their rules, this family was eager to explore something new. I had a role. I was a resource for information about the world outside. Eli would bring out an old atlas and we would look for the places I was telling about. At that moment they were as curious about my world of possibility as I was about their world of limitation.

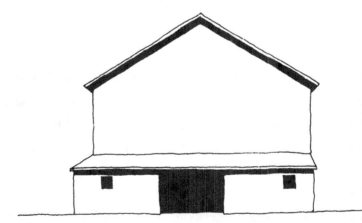

I had come to observe them, and they delighted in observing me.

I never knew what they really thought of me, but I did know that they thought I was rich. I went on airplanes to visit my parents in Florida and had just spent five months in Italy. Eli especially was curious about my childhood in New York and my life in California. I tried to describe what it had been like growing up in an apartment on the tenth floor of a large building in New York City. Did the life I led make any sense to them?

The first question every woman asked was, "Do you have children? Do they live near you?" Most never ventured beyond those two questions. They listened to what I had to say and thought carefully about it. I could buy things and I could travel. But they had the things they valued, family closeness, a community that cared and shared. As an outsider, I helped them to test and then to reaffirm their faith in their values.

Emma said I wasn't at all like her English neighbors because I left my husband to come and live in the home of strangers. I was ready to take on new adventures. When Gerry, the man who introduced me to the Yoders, invited me to join him and two Amish men in his hot-air balloon, I accepted. I was the first woman to go on the trip and was terrified every moment, but I went. From my perspective high up in the air, looking down at the patchwork of green fields, I thought it might be more fun to be an Amish man than an Amish woman.

Was Emma jealous of my freedom? Did she think me brazen to be so comfortable around the men? Was I having such a good time at her expense? I never saw her doing anything unexpected. Did my presence in her home make her question her role or the strict rules that governed her life?

It was difficult to be objective. Emma's strengths were hard for me to acknowledge because I had spent my life running away from the domesticity that was the core of her life. Hesitant in the outside world, Emma was confident at home. Home was a sanctuary—God's home, in much the same way that Eli's farm was God's land.

Emma had a clear picture of the right way to be. It is true that she didn't get to choose it, and she certainly didn't question it, but freed from the necessity to make choices, her energy wasn't spent resisting or doubting her lot. She knew who she was as a woman. She knew that what she did mattered.

The knowledge that her role in the family was necessary for its well-being permeated her life. Her work was valued, she was valued. I never saw Emma or any other Amish woman look or say they were bored or lonesome. She wasn't sacrificing herself for the sake of her family. Making a commitment to marriage and family was seen as a worthy pursuit. All her duties were an expression of her love for her family and for God. The extra hours she spent quilting tiny stitches expressed her love for the person who would receive the quilt.

Emma seemed content. I thought a lot about that. Maybe when expectation matches achievement a person is content. Emma seemed more satisfied than most people I knew who had much more material success.

When I was seeking the special, only a few things measured up.

In the Zen tradition a person goes through years of work to achieve self-forgetfulness. The Amish almost seem to have that quality in their genes. All equal, individually linked to God, each one knew that he or she was a necessary part in a larger universe.

At times, however, I found Emma's humility stifling. It was the same with other Amish women. When I said that something they made was beautiful, they were unable to accept the compliment. Were they afraid that would be false pride? Did they allow themselves the pleasure I get from working hard on a project that turns out well?

One night near the end of my stay, as the family sat and talked, Eli asked me about the art I did. I showed a few of the Amish squares I had brought with me. "What will you do with them?" they asked, their faces showing surprise.

They wondered why would anyone take new material, tear it up, make it look old, and then hang it on a wall? The only things the Amish hang on their walls are calendars.

The concept of art did not exist; in their world every woman quilted and made dolls for her children. There was no reason to single out anyone and label her an artist.

Ambition didn't get in their way. Making a doll or a quilt was no more special than canning green beans or baking a cake. An Amish mother wasn't looking for significance as her fingers stuffed the doll with straw, using whatever unneeded scraps were around for the clothing. No deep, self-conscious search for self-expression went into the making of the doll. The mother's ego didn't have to compete with the object: the utility of the object, not the reflection of the maker, was what was important.

When an object is made to be used, it must be durable. The doll's strength was based on necessity. Beauty came by chance.

Self-conscious as an artist, I learned about art from the silent dolls who said so much and from these people who didn't have the word "artist" in their vocabulary.

I looked at their life and saw it as art.

.   .   .

I kept looking for the outlet for Emma's creative energy. I knew it wasn't quilting. Where was her passion? How was it expressed?

Finally I found it, right under my nose—Emma's pocket of allowable passion.

An Amish woman's garden is never inconspicuous. It sits right smack in front of the house for all to see. Emma's garden was one of the spectacular ones, with masses of vibrant, dramatic, overabundant color. No "less is more" principle here. She spent hours tending her garden. No flowers were picked; they were there to be seen and savored. Emma, who often receded into the background, let her garden speak for her, let it sing out loud and clear.

It was Miriam, who took me aside one day, like a child spilling the beans, and said, "Sue, see what my daughter did?"

She had spelled E M M A in lettuce in her lettuce patch.

I was supposed to stay three weeks, but when it came time to leave I wasn't ready. It would be dangerous to leave when I felt so happy. I'd resent returning home. My spirit was being nourished, and I was calm and focused.

I asked the Yoders if I could stay longer, and they agreed. I worried that I might never want to leave. Several weeks later, I knew it was time to go. I found myself making lists, re-creating my officious *Things to Do* list on lined paper from the Brimfield General Store. How long had I been doing it? No car, no television, no family or work pressures, and still the insidious busyness crept in. Would I never learn? Finally a less punitive voice said, "You've absorbed as much as you can for now. It's time to go home."

CHAPTER FIVE

Coming Home

At the end of my stay with the Amish, I went back to our summer
home on Long Island. The Greyhound bus brought me back to a
Volvo, three TVs, a VCR, an answering machine, a self-cleaning
oven, and a microwave.

81

I came back from my adventure filled with strong feelings and impressions. Everywhere I went, people were curious. Like a Greek chorus they chanted, "Tell us about the Amish."

Invitations poured in. Family and friends assumed I'd be eager to talk about the strange place I'd visited.

I couldn't speak. I was mute, dumb. I could say nothing.

I had seen something, felt something, been part of something that touched me deeply, but I couldn't say what it was. I couldn't say anything. The silence puzzled them and disturbed me. What I had seen and felt remained tucked away in a box with a "Do not disturb" sign on it, carefully wrapped and labeled: "a precious past experience."

"Goody-Two-Shoes visits the Amish," a cloyingly sweet, rosy-colored-glasses rendition of my personal fairy tale, with me cast as the frog princess, now back in her black-and-white world, aware of every single wart and blemish, and with my new friends, the gentle, pious, hardworking, unself-conscious Amish, cast as the heroes and heroines.

Was I silent out of loyalty or misgiving? What if I found the Amish wonderful but flawed? Would I betray them by finding fault? Maybe I wasn't ready to trade my romantic eyes for clear ones.

What if the journey was special to me and no one else?

• ■ •

Five days after leaving Brimfield, I went to an elegant dinner party in East Hampton, New York. Fifteen famous guests were there, each more outstanding than the next: a best-selling author, a respected psychoanalyst, a world-famous artist. Since I was unable to talk, I did what I rarely do. I sat still and listened. I was shocked to realize that all their energies were spent staking out their territory, confusing what they did with who they were.

Having had a purifying experience, I had come down from the mountaintop and silently turned my wrath on a group of people who I would have ordinarily been delighted to meet.

Surrounded by these famous people, I daydreamed about the faceless dolls who were trying to tell me something I was still unable to hear. I knew that part of me would always want to be a star. But this never-ending pecking order would never give me what I was seeking. It was still a world based on deficiency, a world of "if only." No matter how much you acquired or accomplished, something was always missing.

Suddenly I had a vivid image of sharks all around me. I had been competing, without understanding how competitive I was, telling myself that swimming with sharks was normal. Like a shark, I swam alone, never stopping, always doing. The way of the Amish has so much more connection. They're more like dolphins, which "couple" and know how to play together.

Confused, I made a pilgrimage to the house of my neighbors, Ruth and Tino. They weren't Amish, but they acted as a bridge from the Amish world to mine. Each time I stepped into their home, I left behind a world of frenzy and entered a tranquil place. I know that's supposed to happen when you go to church or temple, but it happens to me in my neighbors' home.

The Amish never talked about what they believed or why they lived the way they did. Ruth and Tino had made thoughtful, conscious choices about how they were going to live and could talk about it. I loved hearing their words.

"What counts, Sue, is not the results," said Tino, my dear friend from Sardinia, a sculptor, a poet, a wise man. "Final products are never satisfactory because the potentialities of a person are never realized."

"Then what is satisfying ?"

"It is the enjoyment of every step in the process of doing; everything, not only the isolated piece we label art. If accomplishing is the only goal, all that it takes to reach that goal is too slow, too fatiguing—an obstacle to what you want to achieve. If you want to rush to the accomplishment, it is an inevitable disappointment. Then you rush to something else. The disappointment is reaped over and over again. But if every step is pleasant, then the accomplishment becomes even more, because it is nourished by what is going on."

I needed to hear his words.

"All the stages of one's work have a poetic nature," he continued. "No one gets paid for keeping his own tools cleaned. It is an act of real art; otherwise you don't have a rapport with the tool; then it becomes a rebellious servant, not respected, not properly handled. If you don't appreciate its weight and be aware of the balance, one day or another it is going to hit your finger!"

One day I confided to Ruth, Tino's wife, that I felt her house was a living thing. I imagined the objects smiling, talking to each other, inviting me to join them in a conversation. "Does that sound strange?" I asked. She recalled returning to her home after being away for four months. "I waxed and shined desks and chairs," she said, "and these dead objects returned to life. Their wood almost sprouted new leaves and blossoms. I no longer felt desolate in the house."

Tino's loving relationship with his tools, and Ruth's care and tending of the objects in her home speak of their attitude to all things. I had to go away, to a foreign land in America, before I could see that the qualities I was looking for were here, practically in my own backyard.

．　．　．

Just before I returned to Berkeley from New York, I went to see the Fairfield Porter show at the Whitney Museum. What I saw were landscapes of land and houses and sky. Excitement and stillness were together on the same canvas. Ordinary scenes of daily life, I said, as the tears poured down.

I read in the catalog:

"His pictures seem ordinary, but the extraordinary is everywhere. Fairfield Porter never made an effort to control a painting; to arrange, rearrange, to force things to look interesting or artistic. He didn't try to create dramatic placements."

He painted what was there. The marmalade jar stayed where the last person had left it at breakfast. Nothing strained or contrived. Ordinary scenes, yes, but the ordinary painted with loving attention packed an extraordinary wallop.

．　．　．

My first week home in Berkeley was wonderful. Ready to start a new life, I cleaned my house, bought plants, got cookbooks out of the library, and slowed down my usual incessant workpace. "Simple pleasures can be transplanted," I told myself. That sense of contentment lasted one week. Then I found myself back in the world of black-and-white splits.

I didn't feel at home in Berkeley, and I knew I didn't belong in Brimfield. The tug-of-war of opposing values was starting again. Flapping my wings against my cage, earnestly and endlessly trying to change, to be one way or another, only kept me stuck and miserable.

I no longer felt calm. No one I knew valued "homey virtues." Why should they? They were too busy, and these daily rituals were just hateful necessities to them.

I was now a misfit.

Helplessly, I watched my *Things to Do* list grow steadily more crowded. I had learned a little but not enough. I didn't want to go back to the disorderly and frantic way I had run my household and my life. I longed to recapture the feeling I had doing chores with Emma, Lydia, and Miriam, but I found no way to recover those moments of quiet attention. I wrote to Emma, asking why she had allowed me to come.

She said they agreed mainly because Gerry had recommended me. It puzzled them: "Why would a lady from California want to be in a home with no electricity or TV?" They worried that I would take advantage of them. "We tried to give ourselves up to God's will," she said. "You turned out to be just fine. We found we liked you, and you were nice to us."

But I was left with my confusion. Only in the studio, working on my Amish squares was I able to bridge their world and mine.

"You love and admire and envy the Amish, but you can't live like them," a friend commiserated.

"I know that!" I snapped.

"Maybe you can't bear to believe it," she persisted. "It was a personal and almost perverse quest for a serenity and simplicity that is not in your nature to achieve. You are an artist, and you can't be contained like the Amish. You're too rebellious."

■ ■ ■

Three major appliances broke down in my kitchen at the same time. Since we had to get new appliances, my husband suggested we remodel. I thought that was a terrible idea. I didn't want my time taken up with more decisions and more possessions. But he seemed eager, so I agreed.

I had romantic pictures of doing a shared project. In the past, we had been a good team. Now he wanted butcher-block counters and a heavy-duty industrial stove. I wanted impenetrable human-made materials—white Formica cabinets, white corian countertops, a stainless steel stove top, and a self-cleaning oven. My dream kitchen had to be easy to maintain. Inhuman materials would support my human spirit.

I refused to compromise. I was unbendable, unbearable. What kind of monster had I turned into? Hadn't the Amish taught me anything about cooperation?

"I'll do what you want," my husband generously offered.

When the job was finished and everything was back in place, I suddenly knew what I had done. I had made an Amish kitchen. My kitchen was simple and white. Uncluttered. Only what was essential was there. Everything had a place. Visually, it was powerful: excitement and serenity combined in a way I hadn't thought possible before I looked at the quilts.

The white served as background, a blank canvas, setting the stage. It provided the possibility for contrast, which came from the small touches of color: a small pitcher with purple, red, pink, and yellow flowers from the garden.

"Yellow never looked so yellow," a friend declared.

The kitchen was calm and I was calm. In the same breath, it was also alive. A red ceramic devil, sitting on the counter, looked on, laughing at me, reminding me not to be too serious. Finally I was home, in my kitchen. No matter how scattered or fractured my day was, when I walked into that room I felt calm.

The room is a halfway point between the Amish world and mine, a place where I do one thing at a time. The state of mind I had when I was with the Amish is with me in my kitchen, a small and wonderful miracle.

CHAPTER SIX

Going Back

In 1984, two years after my first visit to the Yoders, I knew I had to
return to the Amish, even if seeing them with clearer eyes meant
disappointment and an end to a fairy tale. How much was real, and
how much did I make up? Did I have to see them as special so I
could be special? As soon as I made the decision, the voice was
clear:

"It's time to complete the circle," it said.

That same day I received a letter from Sarah, the woman who had made the first faceless dolls for me. "Purple martins, sparrows, checkers are noisy outside, with spring freshness everywhere. Our life is going on so busy, and yet unpressured in a sense like you wrote." I wrote back asking if I could visit her family.

Sarah, the red-headed midwife, who loved "catching babies," had been corresponding with me for several years. We no longer needed an excuse to be friends. She consulted her older sister Becky and Becky's farmer husband, Ephraim Beiler, and their children, Benjamin, Edna, Elizebeth, Rachel, Alma, Leah, Vernon, Eli, and Annie, who ranged in age from sixteen to a year. Three weeks later the answer came, "Yes."

I returned to the first Amish home that had welcomed me. Few cars found their way to this small country road in Ohio, tucked between two private rural lanes. None of these roads would ever appear on a map. Remembering Sarah's hesitation five years ago as I stood on her doorstep, I wondered if this family would be like the Yoders in Brimfield.

"Make yourself at home," Becky said and went back to work making tomato relish for the winter. There was a stillness around Becky, a quiet certainty that struck me immediately. I didn't know exactly what it was, but she seemed different than other Amish women I'd met. Something in her quiet way led me to believe she knew a great deal, and it would take a great deal to ruffle her. With dark black hair, white skin, and a solid frame, she looked not old or

young but like someone who is used to being in charge and doesn't need to do much talking.

Ten minutes after I arrived, Elizebeth, Rachel, and Alma took me under their wing. "Want to help us pick melons?" they asked. "Do you want to put your shoes on?" Rachel asked. It was a very hot day and seeing everyone barefoot I had taken off my shoes.

"No, my feet are tough, and I love going barefoot." Walking toward the spring wagon on heavy loose gravel, I felt the difference between country "tough" and city "tough" and hurried back for my sneakers.

Even six-year-old, freckled-faced, wide-eyed Alma was a master at judging which melons should be picked. We formed a relay team, some picking melons, others carrying them back to the wagon, and soon the spring wagon was filled. To celebrate, Elizebeth showed me how to deftly strike a large melon with one blow. Hit at just the right spot, it opened instantly. We gobbled up pieces of perfectly ripe melon with the one fork brought along for the occasion. Then Perry, their favorite workhorse, pulled the heavy load back up from the fields.

We piled the melons on the front porch and the girls sorted them according to ripeness and color. It was the first time I'd seen and tasted a yellow watermelon. The front porch was used as a fruit and vegetable stand, Becky explained, adding that the stand was her excuse to raise a great variety of produce. "We don't make any money, but I love showing the children all the different plants, and they enjoy watching them grow."

It was time for lunch. I looked around and tried to decide how this house differed from Emma's. With nine children and three adults, there was more activity. Although the basic layout of the kitchen was the same, with a black woodburning stove and a large table, something else was in the air. There was an ease, a kind of relaxed interaction that immediately made me feel at home.

After the Yoders' carbohydrate heaven, I had steeled myself for the first onslaught of sugar. Instead, we had tasty, healthy, and delicious food—home-baked whole wheat bread, granola sprinkled with wheat germ, and freshly picked tomatoes and melons.

"I'd love to do the dishes while I'm here," I said after lunch.

"You can stay forever," Becky's husband Ephraim joked. Usually the girls took turns doing the dishes, laundry, housework, and gardening, while Benjamin, Vernon, Eli, and Ephraim did the heavier work in the fields and made furniture. The division of labor was clear. No dishes for them.

The day was beastly hot and humid, and an almost unreal stillness hung in the air. After lunch I offered to read the young ones a story.

"Yes, but first we're going to have a water fight."

Where were the somber, serious Amish children? Not here. It was a truly first-class, state-of-the art water fight. There was no holding back; all hell broke loose. Squalls of glee as the children ran down to the barn, grabbed buckets, filled them with water from the cows' trough, and proceeded to drown each other in flying water. Benjamin lifted Elizebeth and then Rachel in the air and dumped each one unceremoniously in the trough. Even the youngest children weren't afraid to join in, nor were they spared getting bombarded unmercifully. Drenched and slipping in the mud with unabashed delight, they trooped back to the house, exhausted and happy, a procession of moving mud sculptures.

There were no reprimands from Becky. She just shook her head, smiling. "You'd better get to taking showers before you do anything else," she said at the sight of these creatures from another planet.

I had been there five hours, and three stereotypes had vanished: unhealthy food, serious Amish children, and strict parents.

With the girls, I felt like Snow White with the Seven Dwarfs. They all pitched in with good humor. Each knew how to do the chores and was competent at whatever job was assigned to her. Edna, the oldest, was the overseer and Becky's primary assistant, especially when Becky was delivering babies.

Two weeks and 3,865 dishes later, I noticed that the family had accumulated less than one tall kitchen-sized can of disposable garbage. Everything was recycled, and there was an exquisite order to the recycling: leftover food went in the slop bucket for the animals; whatever was unsuitable for the animals went into the compost. The farm and animals produced vegetables, milk, butter, eggs, cheese, meats, and tea, so there was little packaging to contend with. This family of ten ate three hearty meals a day and went to the supermarket once a month. Sugar, flour, oats, and breakfast cereals were about the only things they bought.

Becky calculated how long it took to make mayonnaise by hand and decided it was cheaper to buy it at the store. Ephraim picked Guernsey cows over Holsteins because they gave richer cream, which meant better butter, even though the Holsteins gave more milk.

When they discussed these decisions, it was never a matter of making a right or a wrong choice, but rather discussing their priori-

ties and then choosing what worked best for them.

Change was viewed in a context of what was practical and useful. They had limits set by their religious principles, but once these were acknowledged, they seemed to have a great deal of freedom.

.   .   .

I hoped a baby would be born while I was there, but without a telephone, Sarah and Becky never knew when a mother might arrive on their doorstep. I wondered how they could make plans, but the women laughed at my concern. "We're always here," Becky said. "And on Sundays we take turns going to church—we belong to two church groups, and one meets one Sunday, the other the next." They didn't see not having a phone as a hardship or a restriction. Their rich and varied life was centered around the home. Sarah saw her chiropractic patients in a small new addition that Ephraim and Benjamin had built next-door to the family's house.

At three A.M. on the fifth day, I heard a knock on the door. "Would you like to see a baby being born?" Sarah whispered. Two minutes later I was dressed, finding my way gingerly down the stairs in the dark, wishing there was an electric light to switch on. Soon I met Wilma, an Amish woman, two centimeters dilated.

Sarah introduced us and showed me first how to find the acupressure point on Wilma's feet, and how to press on her soles when the contractions were especially hard. "That seems to make a difference," Wilma said sweetly, as I worked on her feet. I worried that I might feel faint when the baby was born. While I was debating what to do, Wilma, squeezing my hand, said, "Sue, you must watch when my baby comes out." A simple mandate, and so I watched the everyday miracle of birth.

Two days later I carried baby Irene to a waiting buggy, a tiny six-pound Amish doll, dressed in a black bonnet, long brown dress, royal blue blouse, and an apron just like the one her beaming mother wore.

Wilma was the first of nine women to give birth that week.

"I brought you good luck!" I announced. "We broke the all-time record. Five babies born in one day." Hearing myself say "we" felt good. It meant that all extra hands pitched in—a team effort. The older girls washed extra sheets and towels, and all of us kept our fingers crossed that the day would be sunny. Without electric dryers, the laundry storage room looked like a moonscape, white sheets hanging from every line.

The younger girls carried the newborns back and forth from their bassinets to their mothers and brought trays of food—the same healthy food we ate, with extra touches of honey and wheat germ.

Family life, daily life, continued as usual. The children played in the living room, right next door to the two rooms set aside for birthing.

The children knew if they found Sarah asleep on the sofa when they came downstairs early in the morning, a baby was about to be born. I never heard, "Shoosh, be quiet, a baby is sleeping," or "Go play somewhere else." Becky had told me, "I don't keep children in a playpen—it cuts their curiosity." So one-year-old Annie played

on the floor, and someone would keep an eye on her while doing chores.

I had taken Lamaze classes when I was pregnant, but when I felt the first contractions I asked for gas. As a result, I harbored pictures of screaming. Thirteen babies were born while I was there, but I never heard a scream. They used no painkillers, just Sarah and Becky's calm and respectful belief that this was the most ordinary of human events.

Some English women came to the sister-midwives. One said her doctor had told her with certainty that she would have to have her baby by cesarean. She consulted Becky, who thought the baby could be delivered naturally. The baby girl arrived, healthy and normal.

The longer I stayed, the more I appreciated Becky. A three-ring circus could be going on around her and she moved through it, quiet and unflustered. Although she was only forty, she was seen as the wise woman by many women in the community.

With all her responsibilities, she always found time to sit for half an hour to sew a pair of blue jeans or to help Edna with her quilting, using these moments for meditation, a time to be quiet and replenish herself.

In one of those rare moments when she wasn't doing something, I asked Becky how she got to be a midwife. "I started out as a teacher—that's what a lot of Amish women do before they get married, but once a woman marries, she's supposed to settle down, take care of her husband, and start having babies. But I found that taking care of the house and Benjamin wasn't enough."

"I dreamed of becoming a doctor, but I knew that was impossible. I knew I couldn't do both, be a doctor and remain Amish, and I wanted to remain Amish." One day reading the *Budget*, she saw an article about an Amish woman in Iowa who had a birthing house. It seemed an answer to her prayers.

She asked Ephraim if she could study with the woman. "I'm lucky I married a man who is so understanding and didn't feel threatened by my wanting to do more than is usual." Sarah agreed, "Most Amish men are not like Ephraim. Becky is lucky."

She went to Iowa for training then asked a local doctor to supervise her. After four years, he said she was ready to do it on her own. That was twelve years ago. Four years ago, she started training Sarah to work with her. "It makes it a lot nicer for me with Sarah here to help."

. . .

After a while I finally felt comfortable enough to ask Sarah why she hadn't married. "I came close a few times, but I just couldn't do it, although my parents and brothers and sisters, the whole community, really pressured me. I must have a feisty nature—and anyway,

I bet I wouldn't be easy to live with. I'm the only old maid in the community."

Sarah loved working with Becky and being a midwife. "There sure are a lot of tired and sore bodies around here," she said, "so I asked a local chiropractor to teach me."

"You've found a way, like Becky," I observed, "to stay Amish and still do work that's usually not allowed." "But I did have to give up having my own child," she responded. "I love being part of Becky and Ephraim's family. That way I haven't missed out so much by not having children of my own."

■ ■ ■

When I first met the Amish, I thought them brusque, even unfriendly. They believed politeness was a sign of being fancy, so there was no please or thank you, no good-bye at the end of a conversation, they just got up and walked away. Mealtimes were usually silent, but with me there asking questions and telling stories about my life, they put aside their custom of not talking and joined me in "social conversation."

"Sue, do you have your own teeth?" Edna asked.

"That's an odd question to ask." I said. "It's not something I would ever expect to be asked. Almost everyone I know has their own teeth, except if they're much older. Is that different for you?"

"I lost my teeth when I was eighteen," Ephraim said. "I feel much better now that they're gone. They used to hurt a lot." Many of their neighbors had trouble with their teeth and decided it was easier to have them all pulled than to go to a dentist.

Another day at the dinner table I noticed Rachel staring at me intently. Finally she asked, "How old are you?"

"I'm fifty-one."

"Oh, I'm surprised."

"Did you think I was much older or much younger?"

"Oh, you look young. My grandmother Rosetta is your age, and she looks old."

"But I do have a lot of wrinkles."

Putting her face quite close to mine, she agreed, "Yes, you're right. You do have lots of wrinkles."

. . .

"Sue, I'd like you to come to church with me," Sarah said on the twelfth day.

She and the girls were excited about my going and were eager to dress me in Amish clothing. At first I was carried along by their enthusiasm, but when I thought about it, it seemed disrespectful, even though I knew they didn't mean it that way. They were disappointed but shifted quickly to what my other choices were. "No pants," Elizebeth declared, "that would be sacrilegious." I spread out my small bundle of clothing, and together we picked a white long-sleeved cotton blouse, a grey linen skirt, and a pair of Sarah's heavy, black stockings, which she showed me how to roll up at the knee so they'd stay in place. A pair of her clunky black nun's shoes, a little too big and wide, completed the outfit.

Sitting for four hours and not understanding a word of their German dialect was going to be a test. Sarah and I set out early, each of us carrying a large, perfectly ripe melon for her parents, who lived three miles away. "I sort of expected you'd be a fancy, spoiled lady. I'm glad you're not," Sarah confessed as we walked. When we arrived, her mother offered us homemade root beer before we left for church.

There were no cars on the narrow back-country road, just a long procession of buggies and a luxurious carpet of corn on either side of the road.

Sarah and I went to a back room where the women and children sit. It reminded me of Orthodox Jewish services I had attended, with the women out of sight, unable to see the rabbi conducting the service. In both settings, Orthodox Jewish and Amish, I felt like a second-class citizen.

No young married woman was without at least one infant, and most had several. I had never been in such a contained space with so many children. Amish women have eight to ten children; that's the statistic. This was a visual and visceral experience.

Only a few children squirmed. Mothers nursed infants while the older children sat, and sat still. I was having trouble sitting still. How did these normally frisky children manage it?

One pretty woman stood out. The cut of an Amish woman's clothing, no matter what her shape underneath, shows nothing, masks attractiveness. This woman was Amish, but her clothes were fitted just enough to be revealing, and the material was expensive, beautifully cut gabardine, and her shoes were smart black pumps. Her sense of style and the way she carried herself was closer to my world of vanity than the Amish world of humility. Sarah said she was from another district, a wealthier and more worldly community. Her husband was a rich farmer.

While I was distracted by this unexpected display of fashion, the men brought in the long, low benches for the feast. One bench became the seat, the other the table, and the women silently carried the food.

It would take three seatings to feed the worshipers—men and elders first, then the young boys, and finally the women and girls.

The same food has been served at every Sunday service for generations: pickles and pickled beets, half-moon pies, bread with three different jams, four different cakes, and everyone receives one cup of coffee. When I asked for a second cup of coffee, I was told "No seconds." Rules were rules, and in this room everyone obeyed them.

Sarah and I walked home recounting the day's events. "When I was twenty-five, I decided to switch my apron," Sarah said suddenly.

"What are you talking about?"

"Married women wear black aprons, and unmarried women wear white ones," she began.

"Didn't you have to ask permission?"

"No, I thought about it for a long time, and when I knew I wasn't going to get married, I thought about it some more. Then one Sunday, I woke up and decided to put on a black apron, and not a white one. When I got to church, I moved my seat from the section where the young, unmarried women sit to the section where married women sit."

I felt the enormity of Sarah's decision.

My dear and deeply religious friend Sarah was committed to the Amish way, but her strong-willed, fiercely independent nature prevented her from getting married. She had struggled to find a way to live with both parts of her nature, and this was her solution.

How lucky she was to have a ritual, a ceremony that punctuated this rite of passage. Did any of my single women friends who chose to remain single have any rituals to mark such a momentous decision?

Sarah continued, "Even when I knew I wouldn't get married, I was still longing to have a child. Six months ago one of my chiropractic patients, an English social worker, said she was having trouble finding a family to adopt a very disturbed, pretty Cambodian girl. I thought maybe God had sent this child to me."

Sarah asked Ephraim and Becky and the children if she could invite Yung Li to live with them on a trial basis. They agreed. She was a demanding and withdrawn child, needing constant attention and reassurance. Becky's children rallied round her, wanted her to stay and be part of their large family. Sarah finally decided she couldn't adopt her, although she was very fond of her.

The community was against it because she wasn't married, and because they believed a nonwhite child would have trouble fitting into their homogeneous society. They weren't villains, just practical people who knew who they were and what they stood for, and what their limitations were.

Sarah's decision was made, not because of these pressures, but because she thought it would be selfish to give up her midwife and chiropractic work to devote herself to one child. Yet it was obvious that Sarah was brokenhearted at having to make the painful choice.

■ ■ ■

One day seven-year-old Alma discovered three Monarch butterfly caterpillars on a milkwood leaf. The house was alive with excitement. Everyone watched the daily progress—soon it would be time for one of the caterpillars to spin its sac, and no one wanted to miss that sight. The women took turns keeping watch. It was a magic moment as the caterpillar artfully dropped its skin, all the while holding onto the leaf suspended in air by one filament. A light-green, glistening cocoon emerged.

Magic without TV.

At breakfast Rachel asked, "Can you swim? Will you teach us?"

"Us" meant all the children except one-year-old Annie, so ten of us piled into the open spring buggy, with a picnic lunch and two inner tubes. With Benjamin in the driver's seat and Becky and Ephraim's blessing, we headed for the river. The girls took off their bonnets and aprons and went squealing into the water in their long dresses. Benjamin, the only one to have been in the river before, had a pair of cut-off jeans that he used as a bathing suit. In my swimsuit, I felt completely naked.

On land, they were the competent ones, walking surefooted and barefoot. Now they clung to me. I was the expert, and it was my turn to state the rules, "No one goes beyond the shallow water. Is that agreed?"

Soon they were floating, kicking, throwing themselves into this new task. At first they resisted putting their faces in the murky water, but eventually faces went in the water, too.

PERRY — THE FAVORITE HORSE

To celebrate our adventure, I invited them for a pizza in the nearby town. "What shall I order to drink?" I asked Sarah.

"Mountain Dew."

"But that's poison. I don't want to do that to you."

"Please Sue, that would be a treat."

As Perry the horse pulled his tired load of swimmers home, Becky and Ephraim were there to greet us. "It's the first time in more than a year we've been alone," Becky smiled. "Ephraim even washed the dishes."

■ ■ ■

Simple life?

Becky and Sarah described an adventure they had organized the previous spring. They wanted to have a two-day quilting party to celebrate the births of all the babies they'd delivered. Over four hundred postcards went out, and Becky, Sarah, and the girls cleaned the barn to accommodate nine large quilting frames.

Women came from eight outlying communities to attend the party. Some drove cars, the Nebraska Amish hired a bus, and others came in buggies. One-hundred-eighty-eight mothers and 75 children came on Wednesday, and 167 mothers and 49 children came on Thursday.

Fifty-four hundred yards of thread were "put in" (used), and 227 trays fed the quilters each day. In the process of fun, food, and gossip, nine large quilts were quilted, and the money received from selling the quilting donated to charity. The sisters cried when the last buggy left. "We'll never have another time like that!" Sarah exclaimed. My two friends, different than most Amish women, seeking beyond the limits of their assigned roles, had created a triumph of coordination, imagination, and purpose.

■   ■   ■

Becky and Ephraim's youngest child, Annie, was born with a severe physical handicap. "Annie . . . Annie," they squealed as everyone in the family touched and hugged her, never treating her as a hothouse flower, always as a normal healthy child. It was a laying-on-of-hands, a healing going on every moment.

I wasn't sure I could have stayed focused on the joy, but Becky was also realistic, understanding that something could go wrong and "Annie might be taken away from us." For now, God had given them a gift. Annie was their treasure, their miracle.

They had much to teach me about faith.

■   ■   ■

When Becky told me that Ephraim might build a small house across the road to feed and house the families of the expectant mothers, I was shocked and disappointed. I immediately imagined the worst—a glaring neon sign blurting, *MOTEL*.

I saw the tranquil landscape transformed into another commercial Lancaster County swarming with gaping tourists. Becky hadn't mentioned the word motel, but my enormous investment in keeping them quaint and old-fashioned surfaced.

For so long I needed to see the Amish with romantic eyes. But they aren't perfect. Their rate of mental illness and suicide is as high as ours. I saw Sarah working hard to purify her thoughts and temper her fiery nature. She tried to follow Jesus' teaching, "Be ye therefore perfect as I am perfect," and also be humble, setting up an impossible pressure to be both.

I wondered if Sarah or Becky had room for a private life or a fantasy life? Every neighbor knew from the sound of a hoofbeat who was going where. Was everything known? What happens to the individual who has a poetic nature and resists being molded?

But Sarah and Becky weren't old-fashioned. They were two strong, dynamic women who had found ways to fulfill atypical roles for women within a supposedly restrictive system and yet still remain rooted to their home.

They lived with a short cord and lived fully, while I had a long cord and was always tripping over it.

There were signs of "progress."

Six neighbors had pooled their resources and installed a phone in an outhouse structure in the fields. It was only used for emergencies, but it was there, a temptation. A few families hired drivers to take them food shopping. Once accustomed to this convenience, they began to use the buggy only for Sunday church outings.

I worried about what might happen as the Amish mixed more with outsiders and were presented with new choices. I had already seen the change in their quilts. When the Amish left Lancaster County, Pennsylvania, and started new settlements, life became less restrictive. They mixed more with their English neighbors and borrowed their more complicated quilt patterns. Yellows, light blues, pink, and a great deal of black, which had not been seen in the old quilts, was now being used, and these new polyester quilts, though competent, lacked force. Polyester can't make patina. In Iowa, Miriam had said, "Oh, the young ones don't quilt as tight as we do." By 1940 the quilts that had meant so much to me were no longer being made.

Most families still have eight to ten children, but now many of the men have to find work off the land in order to keep their farms. What was it like for an Amish farmer, working side by side with his English partner in a recreational motor vehicle factory with rock music blasting and a naked pinup calendar on the wall? Some families now live in small houses with no land. What would happen if the father were laid off from his job and the family still had to buy food at a supermarket?

The longer I stayed the more I saw my stereotypes wouldn't work. The Amish started out as radicals, risking their lives to change their world. I loved thinking of them as people who still resist the mainstream, only now they fight to stay the same. I pictured them as an "island of outsiders," living in the midst of a society that has an unquestioning commitment to change.

English neighbors who heard me spout these romantic theories just laughed. "The Amish have always been on the cutting edge of technology," one said. "They used corrugated material for roofs earlier than most of us," another said. "They adore plastic," a third joined in. They have no prohibition against technology as long as it doesn't violate their basic principles.

They did conform, and they were obedient, even submissive, but they were more mobile and diverse than I had originally thought. Until the mid-1800s, the Amish were a small sect, living in isolated communities. The same rules governed the behavior of all church members. As they grew in numbers and prospered, disagreements arose. Now there are many sects and many interpretations of the rules. The Beachy Amish allow their members to own black cars but insist they paint the chrome black. One of the strictest groups, the Nebraska Amish, settled in Pennsylvania, and they still won't allow screens or windows on doors, thinking them too worldly. "The Nebraska Amish are like we are to you," Sarah had said. "Another step or two back, very simple, but maybe more content."

Because the Amish had large families, there was a constant need for more land. This ongoing necessity provided an excuse for those who disagreed with certain practices. They could leave the community without being openly rebellious. Ephraim's parents had moved from Holmes County, Ohio, because his father thought the community was getting too large and too lenient. Land is scarcer now. How resilient will the Amish be when the discontented are forced to remain in the community? How much dissension and disobedience from within can they tolerate?

If they slavishly follow the rules, will they end up with a rigid faith?

"Our church decided to let our girls work outside," Ephraim told me, "Mostly doing housework and waitressing. But a few bad things happened, so we talked it over in church and decided to change the rule. Now our young girls aren't allowed to work for non-Amish people."

From what I could see they didn't resist change, they were just selective about what they were willing to change. They don't assume everything new is better. They value their traditions, value continuity, and try to remember the basic principles that generated the rules. If they can be flexible, they'll keep their faith vigorous.

Keeping values alive is a constant redefining process. A living faith is one that gets constantly tested.

■ ■ ■

One afternoon I saw Rachel, Elizebeth, Edna, Alma, and Sarah huddled together, giggling, looking furtive. A "private" conversation was an unusual sight.

"You look like a bunch of conspirators. What's going on?" I asked. They looked embarrassed, caught with their hands in the cookie jar.

"We didn't want to tell you, we thought you might not understand," Edna answered with a sheepish grin. With some teasing and friendly coercing, they finally confessed.

"We were saying you remind us of Ida Early."

"Who's Ida Early?"

"She's a funny character from one of our favorite children's stories. We got it from the library, but it's not an Amish story."

"What's she like?"

"She's always doing funny things, really impossible things, while she's supposed to be taking care of the children."

"What's wrong with that? She sounds nice to me."

"Well," Elizebeth stalled, "we weren't sure you'd understand; she's a little peculiar and does strange things like fly over the mountain and wear men's slacks and doesn't behave like most people, but she's very, very nice."

"She's a cross between Mary Poppins and Pippi Longstocking," Sarah added.

It was easy to be funny with them. We had touched each other. A heart connection was made. I was more me when I joined with them than when I was alone, working in my splendid isolation.

I was sad thinking about leaving, but this time I knew I would return.

Suddenly, while churning butter one day, I knew part of this journey was over. There were no more questions I needed to ask. This seemingly irrational process that had propelled me first to Iowa, and then to Ohio, was finished. I knew it totally, in every cell.

If there were answers, they were inside me.

Churning the butter required a strong arm and concentration. It was hard work and seemed to take forever. "Is it almost ready?" I kept asking the girls. Finally just as there were signs of curdling, the process seemed to reverse itself, going back to liquid. Horrified, I called for help.

"Oh, no, Sue, it always looks worse just before it gets better," they laughed.

"That's just a part of the process," they explained. "The liquid, the milk, separates from the butter." That day after churning we got one gallon of milk, which would be put aside for baking. What remained was the butter; bright yellow in summer, and almost white in winter, when the cows have less green grass to eat.

When it was time to leave, I asked Becky what I owed her for my room and board. Becky answered lovingly, "Nothing. I prefer you to be in our debt."

CHAPTER SEVEN

Harvest Time

I flew back to Berkeley in September. My first week home went
well. "Things will be different," I said. "The transplant can work."
I found a friend willing to bake bread with me. We laughed as we
punched our fists in the dough and swooned over the delicious
smell that filled the house as our bread baked. I felt Sarah and
Becky's spirit very much in the room. But it was my friend's one
day off. That Sunday was the last of my community projects: everyone was too busy. Perhaps I backed off too quickly, but when I
tried to enlist others in these homey pursuits I wasn't at all successful.

I'll never find community here, I thought, feeling sad.

My family life went on as usual, each of us going off in separate directions. I had good friends in Berkeley: an early morning ritual, walking with a friend, started each day, and I could pick up the phone and have a cappuccino or invite someone for dinner, but afterward my friends and I would retreat to our separate lives. I longed for a group whose members needed and made demands on each other. But my friends and I had been taught to value independence, not to impose on each other. If we needed our house painted, we hired a painter; if we needed a cup of sugar, we drove to the market.

Deeper bonds meant creating obligations.

.   .   .

In the midst of this second homecoming, as I tried to make some sense of my life at home and figure out what my visits to the Amish had meant to me, that voice deep within me spoke again, sounding as loud and clear and definite as that first time. But instead of "Go and live with the Amish," it said, "It's time to tell the story. It's time to write it down."

"What story should I tell?" I snapped. "Should I *write about the virtues of washing the dishes?*"

Without noticing it at first, I began to limit the number of therapy clients I saw and, for the first time in twenty-three years, stopped working in the studio. I plunged into the story.

My words told of the value of not rushing, but I rushed to write those words. They told of the virtues of being unself-conscious, but "I" was on every line. I wanted an accomplishment, something I could "show" for all the time I was spending, and I wanted it badly. I held my breath, worked nonstop, and ignored family and friends, acting as if my survival was at stake.

I collected the pieces of the story as I would the patches of a patchwork quilt—not knowing what pattern would emerge. Often, the patches refused to behave. They seemed to have a spirit all their own. No matter how satisfied I was one moment that I'd finally found a way to get them to "fit," the next thing I knew I was moving them around again.

For the next three years I whined, kicked and screamed, and persisted. Sticking with something for a long period of time, the day in and day out doing of it, the living with it, was teaching me humility and patience I hadn't known before.

To my surprise, keeping my attention steady and confined to a few activities built a whole new discipline. A single-minded focus— repetition, order, an "inspired monotony"—wasn't hateful and didn't limit me; the structure brought a different kind of freedom.

Whenever I felt sorry for myself, a dear friend would laugh, "Argue your limitations and they are yours."

I found no shortcuts. Satisfaction came from giving up wishing I was doing something else.

Satisfaction also came from doing the work over and over and beginning to value a high standard—the way an Amish woman cleans her house. I was doing the best I could, even if it wasn't the best.

. . .

Harvest time for the Amish means pitching in. Gathering crops was one of my favorite jobs, and I remembered one late June afternoon when Eli returned from the blacksmith shop and told me that rain had been predicted for the next day. We went from farm to farm helping his neighbors collect hay from the field and then move it into their barns. After a hearty meal at the last farmhouse we returned home tired but happy. The crop was safe. An exchange, plain and simple. I had witnessed more than an economic give and take; this was a spiritual exchange. They were connected.

While writing, all my energy was focused on *my* struggle and *my* accomplishment—never trusting I would get what I needed if I stepped back and let others do their part. I had always believed that good things would happen to me, but I'd have to work every single minute to make sure they would happen. I could never relax and trust that things would work out without my being totally in charge.

I wrote and wrote. All my energy was focused on the work, but it no longer was about measuring up or passing a test. A fierce intention beyond my usual self-interest took over. Friends, curious about my going to the Amish, asked to see what I was doing.

I used to think depending on others was a weakness.

Depending on others became a strength.

What happened was a laying on of hands—a handmade process—a procession of friendship. Friends, one more busy than the next, came, reached out beyond their overcrowded schedules, saw the possibilities, and offered their help. This group of strong-minded individuals joined forces—cooperated. It wasn't the Amish way of community, but I saw these friends as a community of quilters, making the quilt stronger, more mine than I could have done alone.

These were my neighbors, helping me harvest the crop.

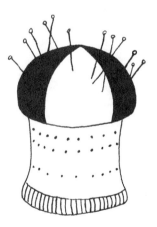

. . .

The Amish approach everything they do with the same attitude. They had shown me that any type of work could be meaningful. It's the spirit in which you do it that makes the difference.

Writing taught me to believe in something and to continue to believe in it, even when a part of me didn't believe. *"STOP THIS!"* my demons roared. "You are wasting your time. You should be out there doing something useful."

A thousand hurrahs for that kind of wasting time.

CHAPTER EIGHT

Lessons

"How is your life different?" friends asked. "How have you changed?" I hated the question.

"Give us answers," I heard, but the demand was really coming from me. I wanted to say, "Look at me. Look what I've done."

I wished I could say, "Simplicity, and doing your own cooking, and washing the dishes are wonderful pursuits and will make you happy."

But I wasn't happy.

"You haven't done anything because you have nothing to show for it!" a judging voice inside me said.

Maybe I should have been content to have experienced a way of life that had a quality that seemed elusive to me. Maybe I should have understood that the splendor of another's life doesn't need to be incorporated into one's own—nor is it possible.

But the need to produce something is so ingrained in me that I spent a very long time searching for answers. I still believed there was "something out there" and if only I could find it I could give myself a gold star for coming up with a happy ending.

. . .

I had picked a practical people who value the "homey virtues." Is this how love affairs begin? Opposites attract? The Amish didn't talk about their values, they lived them. I couldn't live as the Amish, but I knew their spirit was there, inside, and that was as real as anything that was going on outside.

Now when I'm frantic, I feel particularly awful. "Rushing for what?" I stop and ask. It takes time for the "chatter" to quiet down —and in the silence of "not doing," I begin to know what I feel.

My lists are still full, often bursting with possibilities, but I can see what's filling up my life with busyness and what's important—even if I don't always act on that information.

Housework hasn't changed, but my attitude toward the work has changed. Early each morning I squeeze fresh orange juice for my husband, clean off the surface where the juice has spilled, look around the kitchen and take great pleasure seeing it sparkle. Then I go out for a long, early morning walk with a beloved friend. I don't have to try to make these simple activities more interesting.

Before the visit to the Amish, I was proud to make art—precious objects to be seen in a gallery or placed ever so carefully just in the right place in the living room, where they could be admired and protected.

Now, for the first time, I began to make practical ceramics that our family could use every day: dishes, bowls, and plates—sturdy objects, no two alike—irregular, ever so slightly off-balance, hand-painted, crooked black-and-white squares. Their role was to be

useful, but I also liked how they looked and loved holding them in my hands. Deciding which cup matched the spirit of which guest gave me considerable pleasure.

When I had tried to achieve without first knowing who I was or what really mattered, the achievement was empty. Those first old quilts I saw—proscribed, ordered, and intense—told me something about the women who made them and their view of the world. I was beginning to understand that our attitude toward the world resonates in the objects around us. They reveal our intention.

· · ·

"Do you know what your trouble is?" a friend asked one day. "You're more an Amish housewife than you realize."

"How can you say that about me? I'm not an Amish housewife! That's a *homebody, and I'm not a homebody."*

But it was true. Just as home is the center for Emma Yoder and Sarah and Becky, my home reflects who I am and what I value. My house is a self-portrait. It has an aesthetic leanness, a paring down that I have come to appreciate. That spare, quiet quality makes me feel calm.

And it's still a struggle. I have giant lapses—when the house is a mess and I'm frantically spinning, and I resent the time it would take to wash even one dish. At those times, when there isn't a single calm moment in the day, I think of the tranquility of the

Amish and realize I've made a choice.

Unlike the unhurried and even life of the Amish, I *did* want to go overboard, be consumed by a project, and at times lose all sense of proportion. Maybe I needed to give myself totally to something, to feel the ache that goes along with the joy, to realize how much I have to give up when I'm being single-minded. What I carry in my heart is an awareness of the values intrinsic to their way of life, something to aim for.

Finding a balance I can live with—that's what I was after. The proportions need constant attention and readjusting. How much red, blue, and yellow do I need, both in my art and in my life?

. . .

I had been afraid to tell friends what touched me most deeply, because it might sound simplistic, corny, banal. On one of those days when I was feeling particularly miserable, a friend told me about her six-year-old grandson who was helping his father puzzle out how to mend a broken lamp while his grandfather looked on.

"Do you know how talented your father is at fixing things?" the proud grandfather asked.

"Yes," the boy said with a serious expression on his face, "but do you know what he's really best at?"

"What?" the surprised grandfather asked.

"He's best at loving."

Is loving banal?

I went back to the dictionary and looked up *banal*. The first definitions were "trite" and "insipid." I knew that. But then I read on and found "commonness." Maybe the things we share in common are the most important things.

Is loving simple?

Listening to your heart is not simple. Finding out who you are is not simple. It takes a lot of hard work and courage to get to know who you are and what you want.

■　■　■

I never knew what to say if someone asked me at a party, "What do you do?" Artist, writer, therapist, wife, mother—I would be judged by the label I chose. The Amish make no distinction. No one is labeled cook, quilter, or housewife. In fact, standing out would be a sign of false pride. I remembered Miriam saying,

"Making a batch of vegetable soup, it's not right for the carrot to say I taste better than the peas, or the pea to say I taste better than the cabbage. It takes all the vegetables to make a good soup!"

Maybe one of these days I'll be able to give myself a gold star for being ordinary, and maybe one of these days I'll give myself a gold star for being extraordinary—for persisting. And maybe one day I won't need to have a star at all.

▪ ▪ ▪

Following a "path that has heart" offers many lessons.

I saw the old, folk-art image "heart in the hand." That's a fine guide, I thought. As an artist I started by using my hands, making things out of clay. Clay needed patience and respect. I could not will it to harden if it was a damp day. The clay took its time, and I had to learn to watch and listen—to yield to its timing. My task was to reconnect with my nature, a nature that had been bent out of shape.

If I had asked myself at age twenty, thirty, or forty what matters most in life, I would have said being independent and having many choices. But there are lots of things I didn't get to choose: the decent and loving family I was born into; the social, religious or economic circumstance of that family; or to be 5'10" tall, have brown hair, a thin frame, a hearty constitution, or a questioning nature.

When I stopped resisting, when I stopped trying to change, when I trusted that there was nothing missing inside, that I didn't have to choose between one part of me over another, I rediscovered me.

Reclaiming my past, knowing where I came from, getting to know and love my brother and cousins, wanting tradition, rituals, needing to have Thanksgiving dinner at my home every year for thirty years, and being an active participant in a culture that forever romanticizes change is what I am.

"The first principle of a warrior is not being afraid of who you are," a wise Tibetan leader once said. I was beginning to feel what he meant.

And I have another choice—to accept what I didn't get to choose. I could have wished for a calmer nature and on and on, a very long list, but what I finally get to choose is that tiny space between all the givens.

In that tiny space is freedom.

CHAPTER NINE

The Emerging Ninepatch

When I set out to live with the Amish, my life had seemed like a
crazy quilt—fragmented, with no overall order. I had wanted to get
rid of my frenzied life because it was driving me crazy. I kept hoping another image would appear, but there was nothing I could
willfully do to change it. For years I used the ninepatch as the basis
for the Amish squares, but I never felt a personal connection to the
pattern. Then one day, while talking to a friend about the squares,
the image of the ninepatch suddenly became intensely personal in
a way I couldn't yet put into words.

I knew I'd been given another important message.

But I was disappointed. If another pattern was going to replace the crazy quilt as the metaphor for my life, why couldn't it be one of those noble Lancaster County diamond quilts or the stoic, dignified bar pattern? How could the pattern of my life be so ordinary?

I had enough experience with the "it doesn't make sense" voice to know I shouldn't discount what it was saying. So I worked in the studio making more and more Amish squares and began thinking about the ninepatch.

Anything and everything could go into a crazy quilt. The ninepatch would force me to set limits. To simplify my life, I'd have to learn to say NO.

Before I could begin to simplify, I had to look at all the things that were filling up my life. Everything I was doing, everything I

wanted to do, and everything I thought I had to do went into the symbolic pile—one large chaotic batch of desires crowding and bumping into each other.

The pile grew. The squares are storehouses of history, to be moved around, each one changing, responding to everything around it. I saw light in the dark squares and dark in the light ones. The patches, placed next to each other formed a unity—a design for a life.

Those elegant, spare Lancaster patterns would never have worked for me. They work for the Amish because faith simplifies their lives. The ninepatch, which belongs to both the Amish and English worlds, is a halfway place between a crazy quilt and the plain, but for me too simple, truths of the Amish. What I needed for the purpose and unity of my life was contained within the everyday, ordinary elements of the ninepatch.

The world still comes to me in fragments, but I see now that the fragments themselves are not the enemy. If the pattern is strong enough, they will form a whole. It was a fragmented life that I didn't want.

. . .

My work began to change. I drew hundreds of individual nine-patches. Pencil. Ink. Paint. Material. One dark patch, one light patch, a tic-tac-toe grid, a checkerboard. The squares filled every corner of the studio. There was a lot of activity, but this time it wasn't frantic. Moving the actual squares around became a meditation.

I worked with no plan—letting the spirit of the Amish take over. Just as I was about to sew the individual nine pieces together, I saw that the squares didn't need sewing. Even that was too much control. If they were to succeed, they had to just be. The squares had a new freedom. I/we were on our own. When my ego got out of the way, the work had an inner light—something "beyond me," intangible and real. They were mine and not mine.

I no longer felt alone in this creative process. Now I wanted something from the viewer. I wanted to reach out and say, "Join me—now it's your turn to find what you need in the work." I wanted to create an empty space, a "fertile void," as the Chinese say. The Amish often leave a space, a seeming mistake in the midst of their well-thought-out plans, to serve as an opening to let the spirit come in.

I learned there is nothing simple about the ninepatch. The varieties, mutations, and possibilities are almost endless. Looking down at one as if for the first time, I saw the ninepatch with fresh eyes.

I saw a prehistoric marking, an icon, an ancient cross, and most clearly I saw a crossroads.

+

The Amish don't want their pictures taken. I have no photographs of them, but the following ninepatches are the "pictures" I brought back. As I worked the ninepatch in my studio, it became the metaphor for my life.

Each patch grew out of something I had seen or felt when I lived with the Amish. Each patch showed me a new way to look at something I had taken for granted. Each patch made me question my assumptions about what goes into the making of a good life.

Even if each of us picked a ninepatch for our life's design, no two would be alike. Each would emerge filled with the life, the subtlety, the contradictions, and the unity of the maker.

The patches are strong and fragile. BOTH. I'm not going to stitch them together. Nothing is fixed, and there is no right way for them to be. There are patches I'm still working on, not sure where they belong or if they belong. Some patches may clash, some may be missing entirely, and there are probably more than nine patches. Even so, raising the question What really matters? is important. Keeping that question *alive* is important.

PATCH # 1   VALUING THE PROCESS / VALUING THE PRODUCT

All work is important. All work is of value. The Amish honor what we would call the process *and* the product. BOTH. What I saw among the Amish was the amazing amount of energy available to people who get pleasure from what they are doing and find meaning in the work itself. But they are practical people who want that can of beans at the end of the day and the sixty-six jars of relish. For them it's all connected.

PATCH # 2   LIVING IN TIME

Since all work is honored, there is no need to rush to get one thing over so you can get on to something more important. The Amish understand that it's not rushing through tasks to achieve a series of goals that is satisfying; it's experiencing each moment along the way.

PATCH #3 CELEBRATING THE ORDINARY

"It's the everyday things that give life its stability and its frame-work." The Amish honor the daily practices; work, like objects cared for in a home, can turn into a shining thing. All of life is their practice.

PATCH #4 HOME

Home is the focus for an Amish woman. The way she lives reflects her faith. With no special icons, her home glows in every corner with spiritual meaning. Home is as much an expression of who she is as any art work, a place where she can practice what she believes.

PATCH #5 COMMUNITY

Community life is a natural extension of home life for the Amish. Recreation and chores aren't rivals. Barn raisings, shared harvesting, quilting bees, communal singing mingled with feasting—times of celebrating. When the catastrophic happens, when lightning hits a barn, or crops are destroyed by hail or a surprise flood, the Amish face the unexpected with a measure of acceptance. They are not alone to face these difficulties. Brotherly love is expressed in prac-tical ways. They share joy and hardship with others, their com-munity.

PATCH # 6   LIFE AS ART

Every Amish woman quilts and makes dolls for her children. There is no reason to single anyone out and label her "artist." A doll or a quilt is no more special than a can of green beans or a freshly baked cake.

No deep search for self-expression goes into making the doll, and the mother's ego doesn't have to compete with the object. The beauty of the object, not the ego of the maker, is important.

PATCH # 7   LIMITS AS FREEDOM

When expectation and achievement match, a person is content. The Amish standard of excellence is to do the best you can. Their deeply felt religious principles set clearly understood limits. As a result, they do not spend time questioning who they are or where they belong. Accepting who they are brings a different kind of freedom.

Having limits, subtracting distractions, making a commitment to do what you do well, brings a new kind of intensity.

PATCH # 8   POWER OF CONTRAST

It's the startling balance of one kind of energy coexisting with a very different one that captured my imagination: the austere simplicity of the freshly painted white house with its thin black trim contrasted with the vitality of Emma's garden exploding with unexpected luscious hot colors.

The spartan geometric quilt designs softened by feathery, organic shapes of tiny dark quilting stitches make the whole surface come alive.

PATCH # 9   CHOICE

Before I went to the Amish, I thought that the more choices I had, the luckier I'd be. But there is a big difference between having many choices and making a choice. Making a choice—declaring what is essential—creates a framework for a life that eliminates many choices but gives meaning to the things that remain. Satisfaction comes from giving up wishing I was somewhere else or doing something else.

■ ■ ■

When I started this journey, I didn't know my soul was starving. A tremendous need for something led my spirit, guiding me in ways I often didn't understand, and didn't need to understand.

This quilt will tell my children something about the life I lived and the things I came to value. The Amish keep the borders of their quilts closed. *Mine must remain open.*

If the quilt is to come to life, if my life is to come to life, I must leave room for the unexpected.

The biggest surprise—and it came as a great revelation—was understanding that whatever happens, no matter how catastrophic or wonderful, it's just another patch. There are times when something special happens: a marriage, graduation, or the birth of a child. There's no denying it's a glorious patch. It might even be a *red* patch—the one that pulls the whole quilt together. But I couldn't stop repeating, "It's just another patch."

"Life's all about moving your patches around," I laughed.

The next spring I went back East to the house on Red Dirt Road in Long Island that my husband had designed twenty-five years before. I was coming back in the quiet season, before the onslaught of summer traffic jams, beautiful people, and lines at the supermarket.

143

The spirit of the Amish was all around.

Unexpectedly, I started cleaning. After twenty-four years and long winters unattended, the house felt neglected. I wrote and cleaned and cleaned and wrote, and somehow the two were connected. I got into corners, emptied cabinets, scrubbed walls, washed windows, polished floors, and loved every minute of it. Far from being a diversion, the housework supported me as I wrote. What do I really need? And out went more and more things. Simpler and simpler.

Stripped down, pared down, the house came alive. Nothing changed and everything changed. Nothing special and everything special.

Taking care of my home was no longer a chore. Like a Zen monk, raking the white pebbles at the temple, I spent seven minutes each morning sweeping the black floor. A meditation.

A friend was horrified. "What are you becoming? An ordinary housewife?"

Could I explain it to her?

I had always devalued Hestia, the peaceful goddess of the hearth. I thought poor, dull Hestia, the ugly duckling goddess, was stuck by the hearth, while my favorites, Athena and Artemis, were out there in the world, slaying dragons.

But when I learned that the Latin word for hearth is focus, something clicked.

Sweeping the floor or doing the dishes is the outer form, the thing to which I attached myself in order to learn. What I had been looking for was the calm and focus I felt when I was with the Amish doing the dishes. It was a state of mind I was after.

No wonder that "way of being" was elusive and fluttery, so hard to grab hold of. My addiction to activity had diverted me from looking inside, fearing the emptiness I would find. Yet, beneath all the frenzy was the very thing, that inner calm I was seeking.

The Amish had found an answer to the question, "How can I live a good life?" They modeled another way to be. Their view of the world is different than mine, so they reached different conclusions about how to live. Their conclusions are not THE WAY, but one way—a way that works for them. Their life is a celebration of the ordinary.

The Amish taught me something about the human costs when old values are cast aside, sacrificed for "success." Now I am ready to ask: "Am I a successful human being, not only a success?"

My task is to simplify and then go deeper, making a commitment to what remains. That's what I've been after. To care and polish what remains till it glows and comes alive from loving care.

Without wanting to admit it to myself, I had hoped that if I could learn the secret of the Amish life of "no frills," it would help me make great art. But their secret is there aren't any secrets. They know there is nothing "out there," just the "timeless present." Through them I am learning not to rush through life in order to get the goodies. Their way of life delivers the goods, and that is quite different.

How they live reflects what they believe. Their life is their art.

. . .

But the Amish aren't perfect, though I had seen them for so long with romantic eyes. I couldn't be Amish, and I don't want to be Amish, but I had a chance to observe a way of life that nurtures contentment.

The need to be special and stand out, the need for communality, to be part of the whole, the hunger to belong, to be one among the many—these equally competing, conflicting values are all part of me. All the contradictions are still there. I still feel the pulls. I don't want to go and live on a farm, but I long for a simpler life. To reconcile these seeming opposites, to see them as *both*, not one or the other, is my constant challenge.

The Amish love the Sunshine and Shadow quilt pattern. It shows two sides—the dark and light, spirit and form—and the challenge of bringing the two into a larger unity. It's not a choice between extremes: conformity or freedom, discipline or imagination, acceptance or doubt, humility or a raging ego. It's a balancing act that includes opposites.

It's time to celebrate the life I do have. Piecing together the para-dox—making peace with the paradox, to find a balance in some larger sense so that a life can feel whole—with the pieces I have.

. . .

The hardest times have been when it looks as though nothing is happening, or, worse, when it looks as though something is defi-nitely wrong in my life. "It's not working," I say to myself. Then I remember the scrap pile filled with odd pieces of material of those early quilters. Nothing was wasted. Out came those glorious quilts. I have to keep reminding myself that nothing I am doing is wasted time. I may not understand or like what is happening, but I can begin to appreciate that the impasse is another marker on the way.

It took me a very long time to discover that I didn't need reasons for doing what I did. I don't have to explain, or convince, or come up with answers for what happened. I went on this journey because I had to. Learning to follow your heart is reason enough.

To follow "a path that has heart," to take it wherever it leads, is not an Amish value, but it is a way I've come to value. I set out on an unfamiliar path toward an unknown conclusion. Although I didn't know it at the time, I was hoping for answers, but I kept finding my way back to the question: *What really matters?*

■ ■ ■

This isn't a story about miracles, instant transformations, or happy endings. My journey to the Amish did not deliver a big truth. I'm not radically different. No one stopped me on the street and said, "Sue, I don't recognize you. What happened?"

I had hoped for a clean slate, imagined the old me magically disappearing and a totally new me in its place. That didn't happen. Nothing of the old me disappeared. I found an old me, a new me, an imperfect me, and the beginning of a new acceptance of all the me's.

What I was learning was never what I expected. What I am learning doesn't stay with me all the time; but I have glimpses, then it slips away. When I started this journey, I had a picture of the right way to be and the right things to do. Living with the Amish changed all that. Now this quilt, this book, this life is teaching me to trust, no matter what life turns out to be—even if it is not what I expected, or what I thought I wanted.

And I am not wise. Not knowing, and learning to be comfortable with not knowing, is a great discovery.

Miracles come after a lot of hard work.

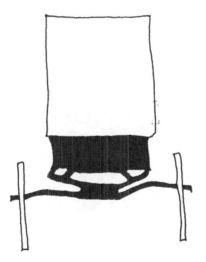

ACKNOWLEDGMENTS

"Follow your inner heart and the world moves in and helps," Joseph Campbell said. That's what it has felt like. A lot of people helped. I have a long *list*. Along the way a community formed—old and new friends—and in the process it became "our journey."

It began with Mitzi McClosky. She believed in me. And she believed in the project. Mitzi, I am deeply grateful.

Structure was not a word in my vocabulary till I met Kitsi Waterson. She and Lee Gruzen read the chaotic first outpourings and weren't discouraged. Much later I found a new family in the *Design Book Review*. John Parman, Laurie Snowden, and Suzanne Chun knew about writing and were enormously generous. Jim Clark was encouraging at just the right moment. Shirley Luthman, Carol Ferraro, and Helen Palmer offered vision. Ruth and Tino Nivola gave inspiration.

I was fiercely single-minded for five years. Friends—Sid Levine, Jackie Wagner, Judith Shaw, and Loie Rosenkrantz—listened as I tried to make sense of what was happening. They were remarkably patient and wise.

The *list* goes on: Rod Kiracofe, Michael Kile, Roberta Horton, Ed Brown, Penny Young, George Lyster shared my love of quilts. Joyce and Bob Menschel, Morley and Jim Clark, Jill and John Walsh, Ruth and Alan

Stein offered their homes and friendship. I felt real support from Alma Key, Mary Kent, Geraldine Scott, Edith Kasin, Sylvia Russell, Fred and Chris Ford, Marion Fay, Gaby Morris, Deidre English, Frances Butler, Arthur Rosenfeld, Claire Held, Jim Rosen, Martha Halperin, and Joanna Rose, who values family life. I feel lucky to be part of her extended family.

Julie Silber was a source of information and inspiration. Bob Baldock shared his love and knowledge of books.

Sandra Dijkstra, my agent, backed me up with her tremendous energy. Laurie Fox has a rare spirit and I felt her and Kathrine Goodman rooting for me.

And Tom Grady, my editor, my friend—I give special thanks. Watching Tom work I saw the art of editing. I also learned I could fight for what I believed and he'd still be there for me. We are a good team.

Janet Reed gave the book special care.

I wanted the book to feel like what I felt when I was in an Amish kitchen. I wanted the words, pictures, and the pages of the book to speak with the same intention. Gordon Chun made that happen.

And finally to Richard, who has supported my spirit for a very long time. Our collaboration on the drawings added another dimension to our journey together.

None of this would have been possible without the Amish families who took me into their homes and let me share their lives. I am forever grateful.

Sue Bender is the author of the *Plain and Simple Journal* and the forthcoming *Everyday Sacred*, which will publish in the fall of 1995. She is an artist and family therapist.